COUNTDOWN TO REFORM

COUNTDOWN TO REFORM

THE GREAT SOCIAL SECURITY DEBATE

HENRY J.
AARON

ROBERT D.
REISCHAUER

A CENTURY FOUNDATION BOOK

1998 • The Century Foundation Press • New York

Cataloging in Publication Data

Aaron, Henry J.
    Countdown to reform : the great social security debate
    / Henry J. Aaron and Robert D. Reischauer
        p. cm.
    "A century foundation book."
    Includes index.
    ISBN 0-87078-423-4 (cloth : alk. paper). ISBN 0-87078-430-7 (pbk. : alk. paper)
    1. Social security--United States--Finance.   I. Reischauer, Robert D. (Robert
Danton), 1941–   II. Title.
HD7125.A19   1998
368.4'301'0973--dc21   98–37325
                                                                             CIP

FOREWORD

Compared to other rich nations, the United States does not provide very generous public programs for the elderly. The basic safety net, composed of Social Security and Medicare, for example, supplies lower benefit levels than those available in Western Europe. But, although both programs are relatively inexpensive to administer, they still comprise the largest domestic activities undertaken by the national government, touching more lives directly than anything else—save the income tax and the postal service.

Social Security especially has tended to operate with relatively little controversy, routinely accomplishing the task for which it was created—reducing poverty among the elderly. Without it, in fact, more than half of Americans over age 65 would fall below the poverty line. Now, however, with the retirement of America's largest generation—the baby boomers—in sight, both Social Security and health programs for the elderly are quickly moving to center stage in political and policy debates.

At one extreme, some are convinced—and they are trying hard to convince others—that more old people will be no blessing for the nation. They argue that America might be doomed to a sharply diminished future unless extreme steps are taken to change the way we provide for our aged. Others advise a more moderate course, adjusting burdens and benefits within the framework of the existing system. Not surprisingly, the differences in approach often reflect a fundamental divergence on general questions about the proper role of government and about the interaction between market capitalism and the lives of individual citizens.

These competing ideas about how to make the necessary adjustments in retirement programs thus have become staples in broader public policy conversations in Washington and across the nation. The outcome is far from settled.

Overall, however, it seems clear that while societies everywhere are converging in a belief that high rates of economic growth and long-term prosperity are possible only with free markets, they also are learning (or, in the case of the United States, relearning) lessons about the risks that accompany free enterprise. These lessons underscore the continuing importance of building strong, democratic governmental institutions to enforce the rules of the game and to deal with the abuses of the marketplace. Moreover, the unavoidable uncertainty about the long-term outcome for any individual of a lifetime of work, savings, and investment confirms the indispensability of a reliable social safety net, especially for the young and old.

With so much at stake for so many, The Century Foundation/ Twentieth Century Fund has been supporting and publishing a wide array of analyses of the aging of America. On Social Security alone, we have published Robert M. Ball's *Straight Talk about Social Security;* Robert Eisner's *Social Security: More, Not Less;* multiple editions of our extremely popular Basics pamphlet, *Social Security Reform;* and we have set up a website providing information on this critical issue: www.socsec.org. We have been joined in our efforts by other organizations and individuals whose work has added to our understanding of the issues involved in retirement security.

In these efforts, a few experts stand out as exceptional for the breadth and depth of their knowledge and the fairness of their approach. Henry J. Aaron and Robert D. Reischauer of the Brookings Institution are in this elite class. The opportunity to make possible the publication of their analysis and conclusions about how to save Social Security is one of the high points of our efforts to bring more light to this important debate. In the pages that follow, Aaron and Reischauer clearly lay out the basics about the impact of the boomers on the Social Security system. They sort through the major proposals that have been made to deal with the challenge of more elderly. And in an objective but blunt fashion, they assess the strengths and weaknesses of each alternative. Finally, they make a compelling case for their own synthesis of the best elements of a reform program. In one volume, in other words, there is just about everything an informed citizen needs to know about what is right and what is wrong with Social Security and how to preserve the system for the future.

In the end, of course, the authors stress that there is no magic formula that will sweep away all the issues raised by the aging of the boomers. For all but a few fortunate individuals, as well as for the nation as a whole, many questions (like life's risks in general) cannot be wished or legislated away. Given the long-term nature of the implicit contract involved in a retirement program (perhaps sixty years from the start of work to the end of life), such risks are inevitable. Over such a span, birthrates and medical progress are unpredictable, securities markets are sure to experience immense volatility, and even the most stable democracies are likely to experience sweeping transformations in politics and policy. In other words, the future development of society will remain complex and uncertain. When combined with the uncertainties intrinsic to the careers and health of individual workers, the case that the authors make for a safe and conservative social insurance program seems eminently sensible.

Social Security is far from perfect, but as the old joke reminds us, it—like old age itself—has a considerable edge over the alternatives. On behalf of the Trustees of The Century Foundation, I thank Henry Aaron and Robert Reischauer for their exceptional contribution to our thinking about how to save Social Security.

RICHARD C. LEONE, PRESIDENT
The Century Foundation
October 1998

CONTENTS

LIST OF BOXES

LIST OF FIGURES AND TABLES

ACKNOWLEDGMENTS

The authors wish to thank Robert Ball, Barry Bosworth, Gary Burtless, Peter Diamond, William Gale, Edward M. Gramlich, and Jack Triplett for reviewing drafts of the manuscript and making helpful suggestions. Jason Altman, Felicitie Bell, Bob Bonnette, Claudia Goldin, Kenneth Keppel, Helen Lazenby, Olivia Mitchell, Steve Ruggles, and Joshua Weiner provided guidance on data sources. Stephen Goss of the Social Security Administration provided the actuarial estimates that appear in Chapter 6. Stacie Carney, Jennifer Eichberger, Amanda Packel, Shanna Rose, and Jim Sly provided research assistance and fact checking. Kathleen Elliott Yinug provided secretarial support.

1

INTRODUCTION

It is 12:01 A.M.—the dawning of the year 2008. Champagne corks are popping around the nation. Lovers of all ages are embracing to the strains of "Auld Lang Syne," just as they have done at countless past New Year celebrations. Few, one hopes, are worrying about tomorrow. It is a moment when no one, not even the most addicted policy wonk, is concentrating on 2008—the year when a development that some commentators have called a demographic tidal wave will begin to sweep the nation.

But starting in 2008, the oldest of the baby boomers will become eligible for Social Security retirement benefits. Three years later they will begin to sign up for Medicare. By the time all the boomers—those born between 1946 and 1964—have retired, roughly three decades later, more than 70 million former workers will have become Social Security beneficiaries.

Or will they? Most Americans say they have little or no confidence in Social Security, and more than half of young people do not believe they will receive any benefits from the program when they retire (see Box 1–1, page 2). Many citizens are convinced that paying pensions to baby boomers under the current Social Security system will be unaffordable. But polls also report that Americans strongly support the program and more want to sustain Social Security or even increase benefits than want to cut them.

1

		BOX 1–1		
		PUBLIC OPINION ABOUT SOCIAL SECURITY		

The public's views about Social Security have been examined more thoroughly and over a longer period than those of any other government program. Here are some typical questions and responses from recent public opinion polls.

1. How much confidence do you have in the future of the Social Security system?[a]

			AGE		
	All	18–29	30–49	50–64	over 64
Very confident	8%	4%	4%	10%	20%
Somewhat confident	28	29	20	31	42
Not too confident	36	36	40	39	26
Not at all confident	27	30	36	19	9

2. Do you believe you will receive any Social Security benefits after you reach retirement age?[b]

	Generation X (under age 34)	Pre-retirees (over age 52)
Yes	43%	83%
No	52	10
Don't know	5	6

3. Do you think that payments to people on Social Security are too high, too low, or about right?[a]

			AGE		
	All	18–29	30–49	50–64	over 64
Too high	4%	5%	5%	3%	5%
Too low	44	40	49	38	35
About right	38	40	40	39	26

4. As members of Congress try to decide which programs should be cut to balance the budget, which of these statements best describes how you think Social Security should be treated?[c]

68% Social Security is a special program that should not be cut even if it increases the deficit.

27% It is only fair that Social Security should be considered for possible cuts along with other government programs that people count on.

4% Other and no opinion.

a. DYG, Inc., "Social Security and Medicare Anniversary Research: A Study of Public Values and Attitudes," July 11, 1995. Responses exclude "Not sure/Don't know."
b. Dallas L. Salisbury," Public Attitudes on Social Security," EBRI (Employee Benefit Research Institute) Notes 19, no. 3 (March 1998), based on Employee Benefit Research Institute and Matthew Greenwald & Associates October 1997 poll results.
c. Gallup Organization, CNN/USA Today, May 11–14, 1995.

The contradiction is clear. People say both that the current system will be unaffordable and that benefits should be at least as high as they are. Young workers say they don't expect to receive benefits, but instead of saving more, they are saving less—one-third less—than workers did two decades ago. Nor is there any indication that people want to work longer and retire later. While the trend toward earlier retirement seems to have halted, one-third of working-age adults say that they want to retire at age 55 or younger.[1] It just doesn't add up.

Public opinion experts are familiar with such contradictions.[2] They are common when the public has not thought seriously about a complex issue. Most people don't think much about retirement. Fewer still have paid close attention to Social Security. But public attention—and understanding—are vital if Congress is to pass reform legislation, as it sooner or later must, because current payroll tax rates, if projections are correct, will not pay for all promised benefits. Social Security is a program that touches virtually all Americans and is hugely important in economic terms. Some 148 million Americans paid $427 billion in Social Security taxes in 1998. Some 44 million Americans received retirement, disability, or survivor benefits. Practically everyone pays Social Security taxes, receives benefits, or lives with someone who does. Elected officials are not going to lay their hands on so important and popular a program before a public consensus emerges on what reform is best.

Most Americans do understand that Social Security faces a long-term imbalance between the cost of benefits promised under current law and the program's projected income. They realize that the program's looming deficits arise from the coming retirement of the large baby-boom cohort, the steady increase in life expectancies, and the reduction in fertility rates, not from program mismanagement. The public is also coming to appreciate that there is no immediate crisis; program receipts and the reserves accumulated in the trust funds will be sufficient to pay benefits for approximately the next three decades. However, *if nothing at all is done to modify the current system and current projections prove accurate*, benefits will then have to be cut by about one-fourth or revenues will have to be increased by about one-third. While those who cry that the financial sky is falling are clearly wrong, there is a real problem that should be addressed. Modest benefit cuts or tax increases, enacted promptly and phased in gradually, *could* resolve Social Security's long-run financial problem without requiring fundamental change to the program's structure.

But a larger and much more important question confronts the nation than how to deal with a projected financial shortfall three decades in the future. It is whether Social Security, which is now more than 60 years old, *should* be fundamentally changed. The program was designed for a nation radically different from contemporary America. When Congress passed the Social Security Act in 1935, the United States was mired in the Great Depression. The most pressing problems were double-digit unemployment and pervasive poverty. Most families were struggling just to put food on the table and pay the rent; retirement saving was an unaffordable luxury. Almost three-quarters of workers had not graduated from high school. Fewer than one-fourth of women worked outside the home. Fewer than one in six marriages ended in divorce, but more than one-fourth of 55- to 64-year-old women were widowed. Few retirees other than those who had worked for the railroads were covered by a pension. Private financial institutions were shaky and financial markets were unstable and underdeveloped. Mutual funds did not exist. Individual Retirement Accounts, 401(k) plans, and Keogh plans—the instruments of "tax-sheltered" saving—had not been invented. Few cared, because less than 6 percent of American families earned enough to have income tax liabilities from which they might wish to be sheltered.

Modern America is quite different, and the transformation of the nation makes it entirely appropriate to ask whether the public pension system designed more than sixty years ago is still the right one for the United States as it enters the twenty-first century. The economy is stronger and far more stable. Most families have discretionary income—that is, resources beyond those needed for food, clothing, and shelter—some of which could be devoted to retirement saving. Some 56 percent of the workforce has at least some education past high school. Over three-fifths of women age 18 to 64 are in the paid labor force, and two-earner couples are the norm. Four out of every five families pay personal income taxes. About half of marriages end in divorce, and fewer than 14 percent of women between the ages of 55 and 64 are widowed. A bit over half of all workers are covered by an employer- or union-sponsored pension plan. Financial institutions, although still volatile, are strong and markets are responsive to investors' needs. Just under half of the population has experience with some sort of tax-sheltered saving account.

The two issues—how to deal with a projected long-term deficit and whether to change the structure of the existing system—are, of course, interrelated. Some advocates of change argue that alternative structures that would establish personal retirement accounts, invested in a range of private and public financial assets, would yield higher returns than could a reformed Social Security system. If these claims are correct, the benefit reductions or tax increases under an alternative system would be smaller than those needed to close the deficit under the current structure.

WHY YOU SHOULD READ THIS BOOK

Policymakers will have to decide when and how to address Social Security's projected long-term deficit and whether an alternative system could better meet the nation's future retirement income needs. Should Congress replace a program that has been on the books for more than six decades with one of the many proposed alternatives? Or should it close the projected long-term deficit while preserving Social Security's basic structure? The upshot of this debate will affect the economic security of most Americans for much of the twenty-first century.

Almost everyone acknowledges that Social Security has been an enormous success in providing the elderly, the disabled, and survivors with a modest basic income. While benefits are far from generous—an average earner retiring at age 62 receives a benefit only slightly above the official poverty threshold—two-thirds of retirees receive more than half of their total income from Social Security. Without Social Security, the incomes of approximately 16 million people—about half of all retirees—would fall below official poverty thresholds. While the program is complex and deals with more than 6 million employers, tens of millions of beneficiaries, and over 100 million taxpayers, its administrative costs are very low—roughly 1 percent of retirement and survivor pension payments—well below those of private pension and insurance plans.

But past achievements do not guarantee future accomplishments. Social Security faces a projected long-term deficit. Either revenue increases or benefit cuts will be required to keep the program solvent. Moreover, the strengths of the current system should not stop us from looking for something even better. We should keep the current system only if we believe, first, that the United States still needs a mandatory savings plan to assure people a basic income when they retire, become disabled, or lose a breadwinner to premature death; and, second, that Social Security is a better system than any alternative.

Unfortunately, good information to help an interested citizen make sense of the debate on Social Security reform is hard to come by. The current program, although familiar, is very complicated and not well understood by most people. (To underscore this reality, we have provided a few basic questions about the current system in Box 1–2. The answers may surprise you.) The sound-bite portions of information served up by newspapers, magazines, and television are often incomplete and sometimes misleading or inaccurate. Unfortunately, expert participants in the debate, who are steeped in the program's details, often appear to be speaking a foreign language when they discuss reform proposals.

We have written this book to help you better understand the issues involved in the debate and to allow you to participate more constructively in the discussion. An important objective of the chapters that follow is to help you tune up your "BS meter," the instrument all sensibly skeptical observers should keep handy when listening to debates on complex and politically charged issues. As the debate unfolds, you, as interested members of the public, must continually ask yourselves, "Are the supposed 'facts' presented by the various participants accurate?" "Are claims for the wonderful or catastrophic consequences of some new or old policy plausible?" and "Which of the sometimes conflicting values that different proposals promote matter most to me?"

Both of us have been involved with Social Security policymaking for many years and, not surprisingly, have developed some fairly strong views on how it should be changed. Although we shall not be bashful about stating those views, we shall do our best to distinguish facts from our own evaluations of those facts. So that you know where we are coming from and where we are heading, we provide, in the balance of this chapter, a summary of our conclusions.

DO WE REALLY NEED
MANDATORY SOCIAL INSURANCE?

Almost without exception, government pension schemes throughout the world force workers to pay taxes on their earnings when they are employed in return for pensions when they retire, become disabled, or

BOX 1–2
SOME BASIC FACTS ABOUT SOCIAL SECURITY

The vast majority of Americans have only a general familiarity with Social Security. They know that payroll taxes are deducted from their paychecks while they work to support the program and that they can receive benefits after they reach age 62, benefits that are adjusted each year to compensate for inflation. Beyond these facts, the program is pretty much a mystery for most until they approach retirement.

The following five questions test your knowledge of the level and structure of the program's benefits. Don't feel embarrassed if you don't have the faintest idea how to respond to these questions; even most policy analysts can't come close to providing correct answers.

1. What were the *average* earnings of workers covered by Social Security in 1998? What would the benefits be of a worker who earned this amount in 1998 if he or she retired at age 62 after working steadily for thirty-five years at the average wage?

    Answer: Average earnings in 1998 were just under $28,000. The benefit paid to a worker at age 62 whose earnings placed him or her at the same relative position in the earnings distribution in every year of a thirty-five-year career would be $780 per month.

2. How much would this worker receive if he or she did not apply for benefits at age 62 and kept working at the average wage until age 65?

    Answer: The worker would receive a benefit increased 25 percent to take account of the delay in payment, raising the benefit from $780 per month to $975, plus any cost-of-living adjustments that were awarded to retirees.

3. Would Social Security provide a benefit to the individual's spouse even if that spouse had never worked for pay or contributed a penny in payroll taxes?

    Answer: Yes. The spouse would receive a benefit equal to half of the worker's benefit while the worker was alive and equal to the worker's benefit after the worker died.

4. What benefit, if any, would the worker receive if he or she applied for benefits at age 62 but continued to work and earned $25,000 during the next year?

    Answer: The individual's benefit would be cut from $780 per month to $118 per month, but after the worker stopped working when he or she was age 63, the benefit would be permanently increased to approximately $830 a month for as long as the worker lived. This increase would also extend to widow's benefits for the worker's surviving spouse.

5. A woman marries a man when she is 20 and divorces him when she is 40. When she reaches retirement age, does she receive any pension benefit as a result of that marriage?

    Answer: Yes. If she is not married, she will receive a retirement benefit equal to the larger of the benefit based on her past earnings or 50 percent of the benefit payable to any former spouse to whom she had been married for at least ten years. If she is married, she will receive a benefit based on her past earnings or 50 percent of the benefit payable to her current spouse.

die leaving dependent children and spouses. Such programs, under which workers' contributions entitle them to future benefits, are called "social insurance." Usually, social insurance pensions are provided as annuities—a stream of income paid each year to the retiree and spouse until they die or to the family of the disabled or deceased worker until it is no longer needed.

Everyone understands that it is important for workers to save for retirement and to protect themselves or their dependents against the earnings loss from premature death or disability. But now that most have some discretionary income, some observers wonder why workers should not decide for themselves how much, when, and in what form to save and to protect themselves and their families from catastrophes. Rather remarkably, almost no one advocates making such saving entirely voluntary. Political liberals, conservatives, and even libertarians recognize that retirement, disability, and survivor pension schemes must be mandatory for two reasons.

MYOPIA

First, most people would save too little voluntarily to finance retirement or to sustain family income if they become disabled or die prematurely. Most of us find it hard to save. Our reasons—or perhaps excuses—are numerous and often quite imaginative. We tend to regard saving much as St. Augustine regarded virtue when he was young and wild: "Give me chastity and continence," he said, "but not just now." When it comes to saving, people tell themselves they can wait—"until next year," "until the car has been paid off," "until that long-awaited promotion comes through," "until the kids have finished college"—in short, "until later." We must buy now to keep up with, or ahead of, the Joneses or for the pleasures consumption gives us, our children, or our spouses. These satisfactions are tangible, immediate, and real, while our future wants are faint and distant visions in our imagination. Hundreds, if not thousands, of advertisements urge us to buy now—and we do.

In short, saving is hard. If you think this is not your problem, answer the question posed in Box 1–3. That exercise will show why most people need some external restraints to help them resist the temptation to consume more of their income now than is consistent with saving enough to provide for the future.

Box 1–3
MYOPIA IN ACTION

Someone offers you the following choice:

YOU CAN HAVE $100 IMMEDIATELY.

or

YOU CAN WAIT FOR A LARGER GUARANTEED PAYMENT ONE MONTH FROM NOW.

What is the smallest amount *payable one month from now* that would cause you to forgo the immediate gift of $100?

WRITE DOWN YOUR ANSWER BEFORE YOU READ ANY FURTHER.

. . . .

If you are like most people, you will want considerably more than $100—perhaps $125 or even $150—for not taking the very attractive bird-in-the-hand.

Some simple calculations reveal that your request, which you might regard as reasonable, is in fact quite extraordinary. If you said that you would accept $125 in one month, you are implicitly insisting on a 1,355 percent annual rate of return! If you demanded $150, you are saying that you will save $100 for one month only if you receive an annualized rate of return of 12,875 percent! Even if you would accept as little as $110, you would still be demanding what is equivalent to an annual return of 214 percent.

No legal, reasonably safe investment can promise to yield returns anywhere close to 214 percent. Most forms of retirement saving yield somewhere between 3 and 8 percent annually above the inflation rate, which has been running below 3 percent in recent years. This suggests that, if you would have been satisfied with what historically has been a very good rate of return, you should have been willing to accept $100.80 for deferring receipt of the $100 for a month.

This simple example illustrates why, if you are like most people, you won't save enough voluntarily to support yourself adequately in retirement. You may appreciate that you are not really behaving sensibly when you demand such implausibly high returns. That may make you willing to let your employer lock up part of your compensation in a pension plan to which you cannot gain access until you retire. By doing this, you deny yourself the option of succumbing to temptation. But you also acknowledge that, left to your own devices, you would not do what you know is really in your long-term best interest.

Unfortunately, the price of putting off saving is high—even exorbitant. Thirty-year-olds have to save 16 percent of their pretax incomes to retire at age 65 with a pension equal to 80 percent of preretirement income. If they wait until crows' feet appear and gray hairs salt their heads—say, age 45— they would have to stash away a whopping 28 percent of their incomes to reach that same goal.[3]

The lesson is simple: Most people *voluntarily* would save too little and too late to retire at age 65 or even 70 without experiencing a huge drop in their standard of living. Among people age 51 to 61 in 1992, some 25 percent had zero or negative financial net worth, and 75 percent had financial net worth of $36,000 or less. Nearly half said that they had thought about retirement "hardly at all" or "a little."[4] In addition, only half of this age group is covered by a private pension, and the benefits from these pensions are often quite modest. For example, in 1995, half of retirees who had private pension income received less than $6,000 from that source. And so, without mandatory saving through Social Security, retirement at customary living standards would be impossible for most of today's older workers.

MORAL HAZARD

The second widely appreciated reason that all developed nations have made participation in their pension systems mandatory relates to the social "safety nets" they have erected to protect their citizens from destitution. These welfare programs provide insurance against income loss. All insurance can cause people to pay less attention to the risks against which they are protected—a response known as "moral hazard." Insured automobile owners can drive with a bit more abandon because insurance pays for damage their recklessness may cause. Homeowners with fire insurance can stint on costly fire-retardant materials when they remodel their homes. Some skiers might take up an orthopedically less hazardous sport if health insurance did not pay for athletic injuries.

In the same way, programs that give income to the destitute may discourage saving, particularly by those who have little hope of saving enough to provide an income appreciably higher than the safety net's assistance. In fact, they may conclude that it is not worth saving at all. Suppose you knew that you could not possibly save enough to provide appreciably more than $8,000 a year—the approximate value in 1998 of the maximum cash welfare payment for the elderly, the bonus value of food stamps, and the subsidy Medicaid provides to pay the Medicare premiums of the poor elderly. You might well reckon that there is no reason to forgo desirable and necessary consumption during your working years to save for retirement.[5] If many people thought this way, welfare programs for the elderly would cause voluntary retirement saving to fall and the cost of assistance to low-income persons to increase. Benefits available to the indigent disabled or widows create the same problem. Mandatory retirement, survivor, and disability insurance thereby help people overcome the urge to consume too much when they are young and healthy and also permit more generous aid for the indigent at less cost than would otherwise be possible.

TUNE IT UP OR TRADE IT IN?

Accepting the need for a mandatory system still leaves open the form it should take. The major alternative now being proposed is a partially or fully privatized system that would shift part or all of the Social Security payroll tax to personal retirement accounts. Supporters of these approaches advance some powerful arguments. They emphasize the current inadequacy of personal saving and argue that a partially or fully privatized system would boost national saving because it would accumulate larger reserves than the current system. Added national saving would generate increased economic growth that, in turn, could help the nation shoulder the future costs of benefits for retiring baby boomers.

Advocates also claim that contributions made to private accounts will earn higher rates of return for workers than an unchanged Social Security system would provide. If true, lower tax rates would be capable of sustaining any particular level of benefits.

Champions of private accounts also believe that Americans can and should take more responsibility for their own retirement saving. The public is financially more sophisticated than it was in the past. A generation ago, few Americans had invested in anything more complex than a passbook savings account and a fixed-rate mortgage. Now tens of millions own stocks, CDs, bonds, and mutual funds, and many carry variable-rate mortgages or have refinanced their homes when interest rates have fallen. Millions manage their own personal tax-sheltered savings plans—Individual Retirement Accounts (IRAs)—that supplement Social Security and employer-sponsored pension plans.

While these arguments are appealing, we think the case for retaining the Social Security system—with certain significant modifications—is stronger. Fundamental to this position is the belief that Social Security provides greater pension security than could mandatory saving in personal retirement accounts. If the underlying purpose of mandatory saving schemes is to assure retirees, the disabled, and survivors adequate basic incomes, then uncertainty about what that income will be defeats the central objective. The need for reliability leads to two important aspects of Social Security that are not necessarily present in privatized systems. First, the pension benefit a worker or that worker's relatives receive under Social Security is tied to the worker's earnings over his or her entire career and, therefore, is related to the standard of living to which the worker is accustomed. And second, the beneficiary must take the pension as an inflation-protected annuity, which ensures that payments will not stop while the pensioner and spouse are still alive and that inflation will not erode the purchasing power of the pension.

In contrast, pensions provided by individual accounts would be uncertain. Even if regulations required the investment of account balances only in broad stock and bond index funds, the resultant pensions would be acutely sensitive to variations in asset prices and interest rates, particularly to variations close to the time a worker retired. If workers could select from a wide array of investments for their personal accounts, as they now do with IRAs, the uncertainties would be even larger. Although millions of Americans have acquired a measure of financial sophistication in managing personal savings, most people know little about finance. Moreover, even experienced investors sometimes suffer large losses from market gyrations or become victims of cheating and scams. Such reverses are unfortunate for the wealthy. They would be catastrophic for the middle class and poor whose pensions are vulnerable to reverses in financial markets, particularly reverses that occur just before retirement, disability, or the death of a breadwinner.

Furthermore, unless retirees were required to convert their account balances into annuities, some might outlive their retirement savings and end up dependent on welfare assistance. And the purchasing power of these private annuities would be vulnerable to erosion from unanticipated inflation unless they provided inflation protection—which is not yet available in the private annuity market.

While advocates of privatization argue that higher returns would offset such uncertainty, there can be no financial "Lake Wobegon" effect. Unlike Garrison Keillor's mythical Minnesota community where all the children are above average, the average private account cannot enjoy a return much different from the average return on all investments in the economy. But a privatized structure would generate higher sales, administrative, and compliance costs than would Social Security if reserves were invested in similar assets. Investment management fees could eat into the returns earned by private accounts, diminishing the balances available to support retirement pensions. As a result, the average net returns to pensions would be higher under Social Security than under direct individual investment and the pensions would be more reliable. If so, the benefits of earning a higher return can be gained by society without imposing uncertainty on individual retirees.

Of course, people should also be encouraged to save voluntarily for retirement and should be free to invest in risky assets. But the income foundation on which everyone depends should not be subject to the caprice of business cycles, interest rate spikes, stock market crashes, or the sharp selling practices that can characterize private financial markets.

Our conclusion is simple. Social Security *has* worked extremely well and can continue to provide assured and adequate income support to the retired, the disabled, and families of deceased workers in the future. It equitably spreads across all of society the risks that people are ill-equipped to handle individually—such as the possibility that asset prices will collapse, that inflation will accelerate, or that a retiree will be blessed with an unusually long life. While Social Security faces genuine financial problems, these problems can be solved without changing the fundamental structure of the system. We believe that elected officials and opinion leaders should fix Social Security, not trade it in.

The specific measures that could fix the current system are not complex, but neither will they be easy to swallow. Investing Social Security's reserves in a broad mix of private and public assets would strengthen the program's financial position substantially. But additional measures—benefit cuts or tax increases—are required to fully address the program's long-run imbalance. In choosing among the many available policies to close the remaining deficit, we recommend ones that would spread the burden broadly and reflect the economic and social changes that have occurred since Social Security was enacted. We propose to accelerate already scheduled across-the-board benefit reductions. So that workers are not tempted to retire early with reduced pensions that later prove to be inadequate, we recommend gradually increasing the age of initial eligibility for benefits from 62 to 64. The substantial increase in labor force participation of women justifies a modest reduction in the special benefit provided to spouses who have had no or limited work histories. To relieve the strained circumstances many surviving spouses face, we advocate a modest boost in benefits paid to survivors. To make the program truly universal, we recommend that the one significant group of uncovered workers—employees of those states and localities that chose not to join the program—be gradually brought into the program. Finally, we believe that Social Security benefits should be treated no differently from other contributory pensions under the personal income tax. These measures, described in detail in Chapter 6, are more than sufficient to put Social Security on a firm fiscal footing for the long run. More importantly, they preserve the basic structure of Social Security, which has served the nation well for six decades and which we believe is better suited than any alternative to support pensions in the twenty-first century.

2

THE CHANGING MEANING
OF RETIREMENT

Shortly before he died in 1995 at the age of 107, the highly successful Broadway impresario George Abbott was asked to recall
the most important change that had come to Broadway during his
long professional life. "Electricity," he replied. Abbott's answer illustrates the staggering transformations that can occur in just one, admit-
tedly very long, life. But numerous equally remarkable changes occur
during lives of more normal durations.

Over the past century, the experience of growing old in America
has changed far more profoundly than any of the transformations
along George Abbott's Great White Way—or in all prior recorded
history. That people now live long enough to share years of retirement with spouses, children, and grandchildren is unprecedented.
Life expectancies have increased from 47 years for an infant born in
1900 to over 75 years for infants born today. In addition, people
can actually afford to retire. Until well into the twentieth century,
economic necessity forced most men to work until they died or physical debility made work impossible. Financial security in old age and
the option of enjoying years of leisure, health, and independence—
once rare blessings of a privileged few—have become normal and
unremarkable. Most of the credit for this transformation goes to
improved public health, rising incomes, and medical advances, but a

good portion is also attributable to Social Security. Before we turn to a detailed discussion of the current policy debate it is instructive to recall what life—work and growing old—was like for generations before Social Security.

A TALE OF FOUR GENERATIONS

A scrim of forgetfulness shields us from a rather ugly picture of what it meant to grow old in America just a couple of generations ago. It is, however, worth drawing back that curtain in order to view clearly the harsh realities our forebears faced. Imagine that you are watching, as in time-lapse photography, the lives of people randomly selected from four generations—born in 1860, 1890, 1930, and 1960. The views open in the years in which each group celebrates its twentieth birthday, that is, in 1880, 1910, 1950 and 1980. Watching the experiences of each group unfold helps foster an appreciation of what work and growing old were like for our forebears and what rising incomes, improved public and private health services, and the advent and growth of Social Security and private pensions have meant for everyone—not just for the elderly, but also for the disabled, widows, widowers, and their children. It also underscores the importance of ensuring that, whatever changes the nation makes in its mandatory retirement pension scheme, the accomplishments of the past six decades not be put in jeopardy.

THE 1860 COHORT

This generation was born on the eve of the U.S. Civil War and turned age 20 in the midst of one of America's most rambunctious periods of economic growth and transformation. Its members reached age 60 just after the end of World War I as the Roaring Twenties were getting under way.

A quarter of those born in 1860 had died before reaching age 20, and of those still alive at age 20, nearly half would die before reaching age 65. Living conditions and public sanitation were appalling by today's standards. Infections were common and disease spread quickly. Few houses at the turn of the century had indoor plumbing.

Few cities had municipal water and sewer systems. Refrigeration was rudimentary. The books of the muckrakers described the fetid conditions in which food was prepared for the marketplace. Health care was just emerging from the superstition and pretentious ineffectualness that had been its hallmark throughout prior history. Surgery was uncommon and dangerous because surgical technique was primitive and anesthesia was dangerous. Immunization for smallpox was introduced in 1796, but inoculations were uncommon. Children died in droves from childhood diseases, and pneumonia was christened the "widow's friend."

By today's standards, the 1860 cohort would be viewed as a generation of educational dropouts, yet, at that time, America's educational accomplishments led the world. Seventy out of 100 Americans in the 1860 cohort finished primary school, 12 graduated from high school, and three from college.

Average incomes grew remarkably but unevenly between 1880 and 1925. Alternating booms and busts made jobs insecure and retirement saving difficult, even for the thrifty. Thirteen economic contractions, eleven of which lasted more than a year and many of which were catastrophic by modern standards, spotted this forty-five-year interval. Output fell by over 7 percent following the 1893 panic and by over 8 percent in the 1907-08 depression. The economy shrank by about 6 percent on the eve of World War I and by a similar amount after the armistice. Just before the Roaring Twenties got under way, output contracted by over 13 percent. By contrast, output has fallen no more than 3.7 percent in any of the nine recessions since World War II.

In the course of these fluctuations, America began to urbanize. Nearly three-quarters of the population of 1880 lived on farms or in towns of under 2,500 inhabitants. Only one person in seven lived in one of the thirty-five cities with more than 50,000 inhabitants. By 1920, fewer than half of the nation's residents lived on farms or in small towns, and close to one-third lived in one of 144 cities with more than 50,000 inhabitants. Just under half of the population owned their own homes.

Families were large—the average woman gave birth to more than five children. The back-breaking job of caring for children, husbands, brothers, sisters, and parents in a world without washing machines, vacuum cleaners, and dishwashers was a woman's burden, borne until death and lightened only as family members died or moved away. Once married, few white women worked outside the home for pay, although many toiled on the family farm. Those who did work for pay almost invariably performed menial tasks; many, particularly African-American women, were domestics. In the late 1800s, men still filled most positions in what would later become "women's jobs"—as office secretaries and schoolteachers.

During the early decades of the twentieth century, old age was not a *passage* to a new mode of living but a continuation of what life was when young. Retirement was a privilege of a wealthy few or a regrettable necessity for the disabled or seriously ill. Over three-quarters of the men still alive when they turned 65 in 1925 continued to work for pay until death, disability, or economic catastrophe intervened.

Such a catastrophe—the Great Depression—did strike when the 1860 cohort was 69 years old. By 1932 almost one-quarter of the labor force was out of work. Older workers were more likely than younger workers to lose their jobs and less likely to find new ones. Protracted unemployment, bank failures, plunging stock market values, and collapsing real estate prices decimated the savings of those in the middle and working classes who had scrimped and saved. The millions of newly destitute soon overwhelmed private charities. Public charity dried up, as state and municipal tax collections plummeted. A few older Civil War veterans and their widows and some retired federal workers received government pensions. Private pensions were rare.

"Retirement" after the economic collapse of 1929 usually meant poverty and dependence on children and other relatives for support. Elderly farmers and their spouses remained on the land, cared for by siblings, children, and in-laws, or they moved to small towns to live with relatives or in group accommodations. In short, the final years were generally pretty grim for the one-third of the 1860 cohort who had survived to celebrate their sixty-ninth birthday.

THE 1890 COHORT

The 1890 cohort also experienced economic boom and bust. World War I ended a recession and gave some in the class their first taste of foreign travel—albeit in a uniform and under dangerous circumstances. Peace brought another recession, during which the unemployment rate reached nearly 12 percent. After 1921, the good times rolled—except in pockets of squalor that encompassed much of the agriculture sector. Then 1929 ushered in twelve years of economic hell. The Great Depression dried up economic opportunity for this class when it should have been experiencing its peak earning years. World War II propelled the United States into frenetic prosperity. Too old to fight again, men from the 1890 cohort helped the homefront economy turn out a limitless arsenal. Women left the home for the paid labor force. No longer confined to traditional "women's jobs" as secretaries, teachers, social workers, and nurses, they took jobs as machinists and assembly-line operatives, replacing younger men who were island-hopping in the Pacific and debarking in Africa, Italy, and the Normandy beaches. Employers, desperate for workers, discovered that blacks could effectively fill jobs previously denied them by discriminatory taboos. Thus began the great African-American migration from the cotton-belt South to the industrial North. The 1890 cohort experienced the agricultural revolution firsthand. In 1910, some 36 percent of young men worked on farms; by 1950, when the 1890 cohort turned 60, fewer than one in five of the men remained employed in the agricultural sector.

As had been true for earlier generations, the 1890 cohort experienced high rates of infant and childhood mortality, but it benefited from steady, if undramatic, improvements in health and education. Just over one-third of the 20-year-old women and two-fifths of the 20-year-old men in the 1890 cohort did not live to see their sixty-fifth birthdays. Four-fifths of this class finished primary school, but only one-fourth graduated from high school, and just 5 percent earned college degrees.

As was the case with the earlier class, only a bit over half of women were living with their spouses when they turned 65. Eighty percent of unmarried elderly women were widows; only 4 percent were divorced. More than three-quarters of 65-year-old men lived with their spouses. Among the unmarried 65-year-old men of 1955, almost half were widowers.

In the mid-1950s when the 1890 cohort turned 65, fewer than half of the elderly had any health insurance, and that coverage was often uncertain because insurers could raise premiums sharply or refuse to renew a policy if the policy holder's health began to deteriorate. But health care expenses were not the financial threat they later became when medical costs soared. Average health care spending of the elderly was less than one-tenth of the current level—only about $625 per year in today's dollars. But the financial threat was serious because health care spending, then as now, was highly concentrated among the few who became seriously ill each year. Those few in the 1890 cohort who lived to their 80s experienced nursing home care—one of the most striking social changes of the second half of the twentieth century. By the late 1970s, nearly one-quarter of the survivors of the 1890 cohort were in nursing homes.

The Advent of Social Security. When the 1890 cohort was in its mid-40s, a revolutionary development occurred—Congress passed the Social Security Act of 1935. It is worth digressing briefly to explain how this upheaval came about and what it involved. When President Roosevelt signed this legislation on August 14, 1935, one-fifth of all workers were unemployed. Fear of job loss was pervasive. The sudden collapse of the free-wheeling capitalist system of the Roaring Twenties had created an unstable political environment. Advocates of fringe ideologies such as socialism, communism, and fascism, and peddlers of populist solutions to the nation's economic woes found receptive audiences. Francis Townsend, a California physician, generated widespread support for a wildly irresponsible but attractive plan that promised $200 a month—over $2,200 a month in today's dollars—to all Americans over age 60 who were not working for pay and agreed to spend it all within a month. Some 3.4 million people joined Townsend's movement. An additional 25 million people signed petitions supporting his plan. At the same time, Huey Long, the charismatic and demagogic governor of Louisiana, gathered wide popular support for his "Share Our Wealth" scheme. It offered a more modest $30 monthly benefit to people over age 60 whose annual incomes were below $1,000 and who owned property worth less than $10,000.[1]

The Social Security Act of 1935, which established not just old-age pensions but also unemployment insurance and several welfare programs, promised both to help ease the economic hardship of the time and to undermine the appeal of political radicals. When enacted, the "old-age insurance" program—the system of contributory pensions for the elderly that is the core of what we now call Social Security—seemed to many a minor element of this landmark legislation. It offered no immediate help to economically hard-pressed older Americans, as the first benefits would not be paid for seven years.

Even after 1942, the help that the original Social Security program promised was limited because close to half of all workers—including the self-employed, part-time workers, and workers in agriculture, government, domestic services, and the not-for-profit sectors—were not covered. If the original scope of the program had not been expanded, fewer than one in four of the elderly would have been receiving benefits as late as the mid-1950s when the 1890 cohort turned 65.

The program's anticipated assistance was limited also because benefits were tied to payroll tax contributions made over an entire work life, so that workers would not have retired with full benefits until the mid-1970s.[2] Under this structure, Social Security would have accumulated sizable financial reserves.

It is easy to understand why a program that promised no benefits for seven years, had limited coverage, and offered meager benefits did not excite the public. Other titles of the Social Security Act, such as unemployment insurance and public assistance, delivered immediate assistance to unemployed workers and destitute families. Even the later-reviled Aid to Dependent Children program, which the Social Security Act established, initially enjoyed broader popular support and stronger political backing in Congress than did old-age insurance.[3]

Fortunately for the 1890 cohort, the old-age insurance program was liberalized significantly, first in 1939 and again in 1950. Following the severe economic downturn of 1937, Congress concluded that the lengthy deferral of benefits was unwise. In 1939, it modified the program, initiating pensions in 1940 rather than 1942 and extending benefits to spouses and surviving aged widows and dependents of deceased workers. Coverage was expanded and by 1960 encompassed all workers other than civil servants employed by the federal government and those states and localities that chose not to join the program.

Congress also liberalized benefits in 1939 for those who had participated in the program for only a few years, many of whose careers had been blighted by the Great Depression. Workers who retired in 1945 and could have paid payroll taxes for no more than eight years received benefits that averaged $224 a month for single workers and $327 for couples (expressed in 1997 dollars). While these amounts were only about one-third as large as benefits paid today, they were one-fifth and three-quarters larger than those contemplated by the original law.

By boosting benefits, the 1939 law abandoned the policy of building large reserves and adopted "pay-as-you-go" financing, where current taxes are used to support current benefits and reserve accumulation is scaled back.[4] The decision to forgo reserve accumulation was not controversial. In fact, most private company and state and local government retirement pension plans held few reserves until the Employee Retirement Income Security Act of 1974 required private pensions to gradually accumulate reserves sufficient to cover past credits.

Social Security and the 1890 Cohort. Even with the introduction and expansion of Social Security, most men of the 1890 cohort kept working to age 65 and beyond. High unemployment and the depressed wages of the Great Depression had blighted the class's prime earning years from age 40 to age 50. Wartime prosperity and the strong economy of the early post-World War II years provided partial compensation. But many still could not afford to retire. Social Security benefits for a couple averaged only about 32 percent of the mean earnings of full-time workers, and this benefit was not available to the many who had held noncovered jobs, which, as late as 1949, employed about 40 percent of the workforce. One-quarter of all private-sector workers in the 1890 cohort were covered by private pension plans, but benefits were small because they had not worked long enough under those pension schemes to receive meaningful benefits.

With insufficient income to retire, two-thirds of surviving men from the 1890 cohort were still working for pay at age 65, nearly half at age 70, and about 30 percent at age 75. In the mid-1950s, more than one-third of those age 65 or older had incomes below official poverty thresholds. Old-age assistance, a welfare program established by the Social Security Act, provided benefits that averaged $293 per month (in 1997 dollars) to 17 percent of the elderly who were poor and could not work. In short, even for the 1890 cohort, who reached retirement age two decades after the enactment of Social Security, old age was far from a Winnebago holiday.

THE 1930 COHORT

The 2.6 million children born in the Depression year of 1930 were just finishing primary school when Japanese dive bombers destroyed the U.S. Pacific fleet at Pearl Harbor, bringing America into World War II. They were on the cusp of adolescence when the war ended and the U.S. economy straightened its shoulders to rebuild a ravaged world. As they turned 20, the cold war turned hot and some were called to fight in the Korean conflict. Between their teens and their mid-40s, the United States economy experienced three decades of rapid growth without major interruption. Real national output per person increased 107 percent, and an avalanche of consumer goods made life at home both easier and more enjoyable.

The 1930 cohort had advantages unavailable to all previous generations. Nearly everyone finished primary school, and seven in ten graduated from high school. In part because of the GI Bill for Korean War veterans, one man in five—but only one woman in nine—graduated from college. Women no longer automatically withdrew from the labor force after they married. Those who left paid work to raise children usually reentered the labor force while still relatively young. Just over one-third worked outside the home when they were age 30, but three-fifths did so when they were age 50. Two-fifths were still working for pay at age 60.

Not all members of the 1930 cohort were equally blessed, however. African Americans and Hispanic Americans continued to spend fewer years than whites in school, studied under poorly trained teachers in inadequately equipped buildings, and attended school with fellow students who performed below grade norm—handicaps that contributed to lifelong economic disadvantage.

If the educational opportunities of the 1930 cohort were striking, the economic achievements were breathtaking. At the start of their working lives, members of the 1930 cohort earned hourly wages three times higher than members of the 1890 cohort had earned in their first jobs. By 1995, when the 1930 cohort turned 65 and left the labor force, their earnings had grown another one-third. The nine recessions that punctuated the post-World War II economic expansion were short and shallow compared with economic paroxysms of the past. Moreover, unemployment compensation cushioned—for up to six months in normal times and even longer during recessions—the economic loss of those who lost their jobs.[5]

Higher incomes, medical advances, and safer working conditions combined to increase the life expectancy for the 1930 cohort. Two-thirds of the men and over three-quarters of the women born in 1930 lived to celebrate their sixty-fifth birthdays. Four-fifths of 65-year-old men and three-fifths of 65-year-old women still lived with a spouse.

As they approached retirement age, members of the 1930 cohort had options and resources largely unavailable to their parents. Most had assets—private pensions or personal savings—that, when combined with Social Security, provided a measure of financial security. Growing numbers of people retired before age 65 once Congress made reduced Social Security benefits available to those as young as age 62.[6] Nearly one-third of men in the 1930 cohort left the labor force before age 62, two-thirds before age 65. Social Security benefits averaged more than $8,500 yearly for single workers and over $12,000 for couples. After 1974, annual cost-of-living adjustments protected the purchasing power of Social Security benefits. Some of those who were not receiving Social Security benefits at age 65 had chosen to continue working, a decision that would increase their benefits when they did retire. Others were receiving benefits from federal or state and local government pension plans that served as substitutes for Social Security.

By 1995, about one-third of the 1930 cohort received income from a retirement annuity or employment-based pension plan, but the amounts were modest. Half of those with pension income received less than $7,000 a year from this source. When the 1930 cohort reached retirement age, more than four in five owned their own homes and most had benefited from the postwar real estate boom that had tripled the real value of owner-occupied housing between 1950 and 1995.

Compared to previous generations, the 1930 cohort also was better protected against soaring medical costs. Medicare, which had been enacted in 1965, provided basic insurance coverage for the elderly and disabled. By the mid-1990s, however, over eight in ten elderly Medicare participants supplemented this coverage with individually purchased Medigap policies, retiree insurance provided by a former employer, or Medicaid. On average, more members of the 1930 cohort enjoyed health insurance protection than did children and working-age adults, 17 percent of whom lacked insurance coverage.

Average living standards of the elderly by 1995 approximated those of younger adults. Social Security, which provided 42 percent of all cash income of the elderly, was the major force behind this achievement. Only 10.8 percent of the elderly lived in poverty in 1996, a bit less than the 11.4 percent rate of nonelderly adults. Among the elderly, however, major income disparities persisted. While only 4.3 percent of elderly couples were poor in 1996, some 13 percent of elderly single men, 20 percent of all elderly single women, and 36 percent of elderly African-American single women were poor.

The contrast between the 1930 cohort and the earlier classes is striking. Members of the 1930 cohort survived to their 60s in unprecedented proportions, were able to retire while still fit, and could anticipate a lengthy retirement under living conditions roughly the same as those enjoyed by nonelderly adults.

High poverty rates among aged widows and widowers signal possible economic trouble ahead. Some of the 1930 cohort will run through their assets too quickly. Some couples have private pensions that will terminate when the pensioner dies, leaving survivors with reduced incomes. The purchasing power of most private pensions will erode, as none are adjusted for inflation and few provide increasing payments. Some of the elderly will be forced by chronic infirmity into nursing homes. Others will be overwhelmed by the 48 percent of total health care spending of the elderly that Medicare does not cover. Whatever the future holds for the 1930 cohort, however, it is a revolutionary improvement over the circumstances of previous chohorts.

THE 1960 COHORT

The 1960 cohort, born at the tail end of the postwar baby boom, is nearly twice as large as the 1930 cohort. It started off lucky, but with half of its expected life still ahead, we can only speculate about what its old age will be like.

Too young to face combat in Vietnam, America's least popular war, the class took advantage of unmatched educational opportunities. Only one in eight dropped out of high school. Half attended college, and nearly one-fourth—almost as many women as men—earned a bachelor's degree. The fraction of the 1960 cohort with some postcollege education matched the share of the 1860 cohort who completed high school. Eight percent earned a graduate degree. But, as in the past, two groups received less education than the class average. African Americans were only two-thirds as likely as whites to earn a college degree. Barely half of Hispanics completed high school, and only one in ten earned a college degree. These patterns are disturbing because high wages and generous fringe benefits, such as pensions and retiree health benefits, have increasingly become rewards that go to the well-educated worker.

The jobs available to members of the 1960 cohort required less physical strength but more cognitive skills than the positions their parents and grandparents had filled. Nearly three-fifths of men and nearly 90 percent of women in the 1960 cohort work in white-collar or service-sector jobs. Nonetheless, roughly one-quarter of men and a small but growing fraction of women work in physically strenuous occupations such as craftsman, mechanic, miner, machine operator, laborer, or truck driver, jobs that become increasingly difficult to perform as one ages. And tedious work in offices, shops, and factories of the sort that makes one look forward to retirement has not disappeared.

Members of the 1960 cohort were offered significantly higher wages on their first jobs than their parents received when they entered the labor force three decades earlier. But pay has risen little since then, particularly for men with less than a college education. Between 1980 and 1996, real full-time earnings of men in this class with no more than a high school diploma grew 57 percent, which was only a bit more than one-third of the earnings increase experienced by similar workers in the 1930 cohort. For those with no more than a high school diploma, one part of the American dream—that sons will earn more than their fathers—may prove to be beyond reach.[7]

The earnings of women in the 1960 cohort are considerably higher than those of previous generations, in part because they are more highly educated, work longer hours, and remain in the paid labor force with fewer interruptions. When they were in their late 30s, roughly 45 percent of the women in the 1930 cohort worked for pay; some 75 percent of the 1960 cohort are holding jobs at that age. Women's earnings have increased significantly faster than those of men. These trends are likely to endure as barriers to women's employment in previously all male jobs continue to weaken. As a result, many women of the 1960 cohort will be entitled to private pensions and most will receive Social Security benefits based on their own earnings, rather than those of a spouse.

With half of their working lives still ahead, no one knows whether rapid productivity growth or tight labor markets will push up wages and assure steady employment, or low productivity growth and competition from abroad will cause wages to stagnate. Nor can anyone be sure whether most, or only a fortunate few, will prosper.

Members of the 1960 cohort have told pollsters that they hope to retire earlier than past generations have done, but so far few have amassed appreciable savings. Only 10 percent have nonhousing assets worth more than $100,000, and 78 percent have accumulated less than $50,000, an amount that would provide a couple at age 65 with an annuity of less than $4,000 a year. Unlike their parents, members of the 1960 cohort are unlikely to enjoy the windfall of a protracted real estate boom. Easy credit from home equity loans, automobile loans, and proliferating credit cards will continue to encourage consumption and discourage saving.

In their failure to save, members of the 1960 cohort are no different from their forebears, who began to save, if at all, only in their late 40s and 50s. When they reach that age, however, the 1960 cohort may find it harder to put something aside to make up for its youthful fecklessness. Because they are marrying late and deferring child bearing, many will be well into their 50s before their children have finished school and moved away. Furthermore, if current trends hold, about half of all the first marriages of the cohort will end in divorce, an event that disrupts both family life and retirement saving. Most who divorce will remarry, but about one-third will find themselves single at age 65, not because they were widowed—the fate of three-quarters of single 65-year-olds in the 1860 cohort—but because two out of five will be divorced.

On the bright side, more members of the 1960 cohort than of previous generations should receive sizable private pension benefits when they retire. Although the fraction of workers covered by employment-related plans has not increased in two decades, the fraction of workers who will actually receive sizable pensions will grow. One reason is the requirement contained in the Employee Retirement Income Security Act of 1974 that pension rights vest in no more than five years. Furthermore, the Pension Benefit Guarantee Corporation now ensures that the basic benefits promised by company-managed, defined-benefit pension plans will be paid even if the sponsoring company goes broke.

At the same time, pensions are becoming increasingly vulnerable to financial market volatility. Plans that pay benefits until the worker dies, based on the worker's earnings and number of years of service —"defined-benefit" plans—are giving way to "defined-contribution" plans in which the pension depends on the amounts contributed to the account and the investment returns earned on those contributions. The proportion of private-sector workers covered by private pensions whose primary plan was defined-benefit fell from 87 percent in

1975 to 58 percent in 1993. Benefit adequacy under defined-contribution plans depends on what happens to asset prices and on how long the retiree and spouse live. If the balances accumulated in the defined-contribution plan are not used to buy an annuity upon retirement, which for reasons we discuss in Chapter 5 can be a fairly expensive undertaking, many retired workers or their spouses will outlive their retirement pensions. Half of the men in the 1960 cohort who reach age 65 will still be alive at age 83, and over one-fifth will live to their ninetieth birthdays in 2050. Of women who live to age 65, half will still be alive at age 87. Medical advances could easily raise these fractions.

If current trends continue, half of the men in the 1960 cohort will retire by age 62 and half of the women by age 60. They will face a prospect that was virtually unknown to their great-great-grandparents in the 1860 cohort—a quarter-century or more of retirement. New patterns, however, may emerge. Members of the 1960 cohort may choose to retire later or more gradually than in the past. They may leave the jobs that sustained them in their primary earning years and move into less demanding positions. Or they may choose to work part-time or part-year. The rapid growth in part-time jobs and the development of contract and contingent work have already created many such opportunities. Labor force growth is projected to slow to only 0.3 percent a year by the time the 1960 cohort is in its 60s. Tight labor markets could encourage employers to make special efforts to accommodate the preferences of older workers. The remarkable flexibility of the American workplace ensures further changes in response to market pressures.

WHAT LIES AHEAD?

Public policy will determine whether long retirements, even if desirable, are affordable. Even if rapid wage growth resumes, few of today's young workers are likely to have enough personal saving or private pension benefits to support themselves in comfort for a quarter of a century in retirement. Like the current generation of elderly, they will be highly dependent on Social Security or whatever alternative system might be put in its place.

Because the Social Security program faces a projected long-term deficit, some cutback in benefits or increase in revenues is inescapable. The structure that has developed over the past six decades could be reinforced and modified to reflect the changes that have taken place in the nation's economic, social, and demographic character since 1935. Small adjustments along these lines made soon and phased in gradually would be enough to do the job. Or the current structure could be gradually transformed into one in which personal retirement accounts played a significant role. In that case, the risks inherent in long-term pension contracts, which are now shared collectively, would be placed directly on individuals. How and when these decisions are made will shape the economic terms on which members of the 1960 cohort—and those who follow them—grow old and retire. They will also affect, in fundamental ways, the character of the nation and the focus of political discourse.

3

KEY ISSUES IN THE SOCIAL SECURITY DEBATE

W hile many believe that Social Security should be reformed and retained, others are persuaded that forced saving through individual accounts would more effectively guarantee basic income protection for retirees, the disabled, and survivors. Fortunately, the current debate centers on just a few major issues that can be summarized in three questions.

- ◆ *How Should Benefits Be Set?* Should pensions be based on what participants have earned and how long they have worked—which is how defined-benefit plans are structured—or on what they and their employers have contributed and the investment returns earned on those contributions—which is how defined-contribution plans work?

- ◆ *How Much Social Assistance?* Should the nation's basic pension program provide benefits that are proportional to earnings or contributions? Or should benefits be boosted for low earners, widowed spouses, and others who might be regarded as deserving or vulnerable? In short, how much "social" should there be in social insurance?

◆ *How Much Reserve Accumulation?* Should the pension plan build reserves? If so, who should pay the added costs of building up those reserves, and who should manage the investment of those reserves?

How Should Benefits Be Set?

Nobody can escape one key fact about pensions—they are *very* long-term promises. Seventy or more years may pass between a worker's first payroll tax payment and the last pension check that goes to the worker or a surviving spouse. When promises span so many years, risks are inescapable. Who should bear those risks is a central issue in the debate. Defined-benefit plans, such as Social Security, distribute those risks differently from the defined-contribution plans that have been proposed as full or partial replacements for the existing system.

One class of risks—system risks—relates to maintaining the pension system's financial balance. If the system gets out of kilter, whose benefits or taxes should be changed? Even if the overall system remains in financial balance, individuals face personal risks—from unemployment, low earnings, low investment returns, sickness, and changing family situations—in short, from developments over which workers have only limited control. Workers confront additional uncertainties when they select a pension plan administrator, choose the assets in which their contributions are invested, and decide whether to take their pensions as lump-sum withdrawals, annuities, or scheduled payments.

System Risks

Pension plans inevitably get out of balance because unanticipated economic and demographic developments cause revenues and outlays to differ from expectations. When confronted with imbalances in Social Security, Congress has typically modified benefits for current and future pensioners and changed tax rates, thus spreading the adjustments broadly across many people. In 1972, for example, when new, more accurate methods of estimating future revenues and costs revealed large projected surpluses, Congress responded by raising benefits, mostly for future retirees. Unfortunately, an unexpected slowdown in the trend of productivity growth after 1973, recessions in the mid-1970s and early 1980s, and a flaw in the 1972 legislation that raised benefits produced deficits rather than surpluses. Congress responded in 1983 by cutting benefits for current and future retirees in various ways and by raising taxes (see Box 3–1 for details, page 34).

Under defined-contribution plans, pensions can not exceed reserves in an individual's account at the time of retirement. Imbalances show up as pensions that are larger or smaller, in relation to earnings, than intended. Variations in the growth of average earnings or in the returns on investments can create such imbalances.[1] The only way to prevent such imbalances under a defined-contribution plan is periodically to change contribution rates. Plan modifications of this sort can effectively restore balance for young and even middle-aged workers—provided that further disturbances do not occur as workers near retirement. If imbalances occur shortly before workers reach retirement age—by a fall in asset prices, for example—there is no effective way to correct them, because it takes some time before changes in contribution rates have much impact on fund accumulations. In such cases, workers are simply stuck with lower benefits. In general, a change in contribution rates has no effect on the benefits of current retirees and little on those of workers who are near retirement. In any event, the consequences of correcting—or not correcting— imbalances in a defined-contribution pension system for any worker fall entirely on that worker.

Routine fluctuations in asset values, interest rates, and wage growth make it likely that defined-contribution pensions will not produce intended replacement rates—the ratio of pensions to prior earnings—unless contribution rates are changed frequently and by large amounts. Figure 3–1 (see page 35) shows how replacement rates would have varied if an average male worker invested a constant fraction of his earnings in a "total stock market" index fund during his working years and converted the balance at age 62 into an annuity.[2] In this example, workers reaching age 62 in 1969 would have enjoyed a 104 percent replacement rate, while those turning age 62 only six years later would have had to struggle with a meager 39 percent replacement of prior earnings.

> ## BOX 3–1
> ## SPREADING THE RISK—HOW
> ## CONGRESS CLOSED THE DEFICIT IN 1983
>
> In 1972, Congress enacted a formula to adjust Social Security benefits automatically for wage inflation. Unfortunately, the adjustments were too large and a deficit emerged. Congress enacted legislation in 1977 to correct the formula and close the deficit, but deficits continued because slow economic growth persisted, inflation accelerated over the 1979–81 period, and unemployment soared during the recessions of 1980 and 1981–82.
>
> Soon after taking office, President Reagan proposed major benefit cuts to close the Social Security deficit. His proposed changes proved quite unpopular. To limit political damage, he appointed a commission under the chairmanship of economist Alan Greenspan to design a plan to restore balance. The proposals of this commission were the basis of the legislation enacted in early 1983, only months before the reserves in the trust funds would have been depleted.
>
> The changes, which dealt with both the short-run, cash-flow problem and the long-run deficit, affected current workers and beneficiaries as well as future beneficiaries. A previously scheduled increase in the payroll tax was accelerated. All employees of nonprofit organizations and new federal government employees were brought under Social Security. Since most of these workers earned eligibility through private employment before, during, or after their current jobs, this change raised revenues far more than costs. A portion of the benefits received by upper-income recipients was subject to the personal income tax, and the resulting revenues were returned to the trust funds. The revenues from this change were projected to grow significantly because the income thresholds at which the provision became effective were not adjusted for inflation. The cost-of-living adjustment for benefits was suspended for six months, permanently lowering benefits for all current beneficiaries. The tax rate on the self-employed, previously three-fourths of the combined rate on employees and employers, was raised to parity. Smaller changes affecting other groups were also made.

Figure 3–1 correctly indicates the *variability from one year to another* of pensions invested exclusively in common stocks, but is misleading in several respects. First, it ignores variability in pensions that would arise from changes in stock values that occur *within* a given year. As experiences in 1987 and 1998 illustrate, these differences can be large. Workers who sold their holdings at the market close on October 19, 1987, would have realized 18 percent less than workers who sold the day before. Workers who sold their holdings at the close on August 31, 1998, would have realized 21 percent less than workers who sold a month and a half earlier.

Second, workers of a particular age would receive widely varying pensions, even if they made the same contributions and sold their holdings on the same date, because of differences in investment strategies. For similar reasons, the variation in returns *over time* would differ from that shown in Figure 3–1 because most investors would not choose all-stock portfolios. Pension reserves invested in long-term bonds are subject to price fluctuations similar to, but smaller than, those of stocks. If bonds are held to maturity, unexpected inflation affects the real value of the account balance. Increased inflation can cause the price of long-term bonds sold before maturity to fall precipitously. In 1982, for example, a thirty-year AT&T bond issued in 1977 was worth only 35 percent as much (adjusted for inflation) as it was at issue five years earlier. Finally, the actual *level* of benefits would be considerably lower than those shown in Figure 3–1 because the calculations depicted there ignore costs of funds management and of annuitization, which sharply reduce replacement rates.

FIGURE 3–1
REPLACEMENT RATES OF WORKERS WITH
FORTY-YEAR CAREERS WHO INVEST IN U.S. STOCK
MARKET AND RETIRE OVER PERIOD 1912–97

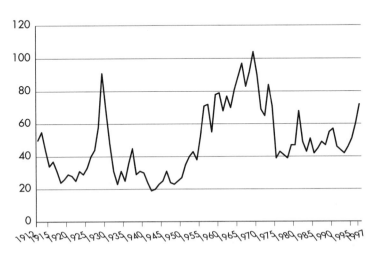

Notes: Economywide real wage growth = 2%; contribution rate = 6%; forty-year career; invest in stocks over forty-year career; convert to level annuity at age 62.

Source: Unpublished figure prepared by Gary Burtless, The Brookings Institution.

Variations in asset prices do not directly affect workers' pensions under defined-benefit plans because pensions are based on workers' earnings. Fluctuations in asset prices and interest rates can indirectly affect benefits and taxes under defined-benefit systems. However, the effects are surprisingly small. Suppose that projected revenues and benefits over the next seventy-five years were in balance and that reserves equal to ten times annual benefit payments were invested equally in stocks and government securities. A 30 percent drop in stock prices would produce a deficit equal to less than 2.5 percent of long-term benefits or revenues. If projected revenues initially equaled projected outlays, such a shock would not be sufficient to push the system out of "close actuarial balance," defined by the Social Security actuaries as any situation in which projected revenues are between 95 percent and 105 percent of projected outlays. In contrast, under a defined-contribution pension, such a drop in stock prices would reduce the value of a similarly invested individual account by 15 percent. The pension of a worker reaching retirement when the shock occurred would be reduced by the same amount, six times more than the reduction under a defined-benefit plan such as Social Security if balance were restored exclusively through benefit cuts.

To be sure, workers or pension fund managers can protect themselves from price volatility under defined-contribution plans, but only by sacrificing expected earnings. The prices of money market funds and short-term Treasury securities are stable, but these securities have produced long-term yields barely above the inflation rate. In contrast, annual returns on common stocks have greatly exceeded inflation—by an average of 8.2 percent in the forty years from 1957 to 1997, and by 11.4 percent in the twenty years since 1977.

INDIVIDUAL RISKS

Even if a plan remains in overall balance, the pensions of individual workers are subject to risk. Both defined-benefit and defined-contribution pensions depend on the level of earnings. Defined-contribution pensions are also sensitive to the timing of earnings, which can be affected by myriad unanticipated events—the birth of a child, involuntary unemployment, a job change, or poor health, for example. Workers who enjoy relatively high earnings and make relatively large pension contributions early in their careers generally end up with larger pensions under defined-contribution plans than those whose earnings are concentrated toward the end of their careers.[3] Timing matters because a dollar contributed to a defined-contribution plan early in a worker's career will reap investment returns for many more years than a dollar contributed toward the end of the worker's career.

Social Security's benefits are determined by workers' earnings averaged over their working lives (see Box 3–2, page 39). Those with the same earnings averaged over the thirty-five years of highest earnings receive the same pensions, whether earnings were relatively high or low at the beginning of a worker's career or whether, for one reason or another, the worker had no earnings in some years.

An additional element of individual risk—and opportunity—is introduced if participants can decide how their accounts' reserves are invested. Social Security offers no choice. Under current law, reserves must be invested in secure, but low-yielding, U.S. government securities. Most proposals to strengthen the Social Security system or to establish individual accounts would shift a portion of the reserves to higher-yielding stocks and corporate bonds. Some individual account plans would also permit workers to choose among a wide range of assets. Others would limit investments to a few index funds. The greater the range of choice open to workers, the greater the variation there will be in pension amounts. Even if workers were limited to a single total stock market fund, however, the variation over time would be considerable, as shown in Figure 3–1. With wider choices, some workers would make unlucky, ill-informed, or risky investment decisions. For example, conservative investors who purchased seemingly safe stocks like the Pennsylvania and New York Central railroads in the 1950s found themselves holding worthless certificates when the merged company—the Penn Central—declared bankruptcy in 1970. Investors who took a flyer on unknown startup companies like Microsoft in the mid-1980s could retire rich, but others who sank their retirement nest eggs into new companies like L.A. Gear, which first sold shares to the public about that time, would have experienced returns well below average.

Uncertainties and risks do not end with retirement. Unexpected inflation after retirement can steadily undermine the adequacy of a pension that seemed sufficient at first. Furthermore, workers who do not buy annuities may exhaust their accumulated retirement savings years before they die.

All Social Security retirement benefits are inflation-protected annuities. The defined-contribution components of most of the plans proposed as replacements to Social Security would allow retirees to withdraw their retirement savings as lump sums, as periodic payments over a fixed time period, or as annuities. Few require payment of indexed annuities.

The importance of protecting basic retirement income from inflation cannot be exaggerated. Mortality rates are falling fast. The Census Bureau forecasts that by 2050 there will be more than 30 million people over age 80 and 800,000 centenarians. The longer people live, the greater the damage that inflation can do to pensions that are not protected from erosion by inflation. An inflation rate of 2.5 percent—the Congressional Budget Office's long-term projection for inflation—will cut the purchasing power of an unindexed pension by 43 percent by the time a 62-year-old reaches age 85.

People who must deal financially with the uncertainty of how long they might live face two unsatisfactory options. They may spend their retirement savings very slowly, minimizing the risk that they will outlive their savings but increasing the possibility that they will die having deprived themselves unnecessarily of consumption they could have afforded. Or they may spend their resources quickly, minimizing the chance that they will deprive themselves needlessly, but risking destitution and dependency on relatives or public charity at the end of their lives.

Although annuities—an income stream guaranteed to last as long as the pensioner lives, but not longer—provide a simple way out of this dilemma, few people buy them. One reason is cost. Insurance companies have found that people with long life expectancies are more likely to buy annuities than people with short life expectancies. Those who are terminally ill or whose parents and grandparents did not live much beyond their 60s are less likely to buy an annuity than those who are healthy and whose forebears lived into their 90s. As a result of this "adverse selection," insurance companies charge about 10 percent more for annuities than they would if the average purchaser had a normal life expectancy. Selling and administrative costs boost prices an additional 10 percent. In total, annuity buyers with average life expectancy give up about 20 percent of the value of the assets they convert into an annuity. Prices vary significantly by company, so that some people pay more and some pay less (see Box 3–3, page 41).

BOX 3–2
FIGURING OUT YOUR AVERAGE EARNINGS

Social Security benefits are based on a worker's earnings averaged over the 35 years in which the worker's *adjusted* earnings are highest. A simple example illustrates the calculation.

Suppose you worked every year from age 22 through age 61, a forty-year period. The first step would be to adjust your past earnings to reflect the increase in economy-wide average earnings between the year you received the earnings and the year you turned age 60. For example, if you turned 62 in 1997, your 1960 earnings would be multiplied by 6.16 for averaging purposes because that is how much average wages increased between 1960 and 1995, the year in which you turned 60. If you earned $4,000 in 1960, that would be transformed into earnings of $24,640 to calculate your average earnings. A similar adjustment would be made for your earnings in each of the other thirty-nine years you worked. The second step would be to select the highest thirty-five of your forty years of adjusted earnings. The third step would be to calculate the average of these adjusted earnings.

Under this procedure, the importance of each dollar of earnings is adjusted by the growth of economy-wide earnings between the year the earnings were received and the year the worker turns age 60. In contrast, the importance of each dollar contributed to a defined-contribution pension plan grows at the rate earned by the plan's investments. Early earnings count more heavily under a defined-contribution plan than under Social Security if the investment return exceeds the growth rate of earnings per worker. Historically, this has been the case, and the Social Security Administration projects a similar pattern for the future. The projections suggest that the real interest rate on government securities will average 2.8 percent, while real earnings per worker will grow 0.9 percent annually. If history is any guide, real returns on private equities will be two or three times that on government securities.

Under such assumptions, the loss of earnings early in one's career will reduce one's lifetime pension in a defined-contribution system proportionately more than it will under Social Security. In contrast, early retirement will reduce pensions proportionately more under Social Security than under a defined-contribution system. There is an important exception to this general rule. If one becomes disabled under a defined-contribution plan, payments into one's pension fund cease. Social Security contains a "disability freeze," which means that if one becomes disabled, the number of years of earnings counted in computing retirement benefits is reduced to take account of the shortened working life. As a result, the Social Security retirement benefits that a disabled worker eventually receives are not affected by the years of zero earnings after the onset of disability.

In principle, insurance companies could ask for information that would let them estimate how long each annuity purchaser might live and charge those with shorter life expectancies less than others. Such information would be imperfect at best, however, and legal restrictions limit such price discrimination. In practice, insurance companies charge people of the same age and sex the same price for an annuity.[4]

Until recently, insurance companies were unwilling to offer private annuities that eliminated the risk of inflation primarily because no inflation-indexed securities were available to reduce their risk. Bonds have not filled the need because their yields have proven to be poor indicators of future inflation. During the two decades from 1976 through 1996, the forecast of inflation over the succeeding 10 years implicit in bond prices differed from actual inflation by more than 50 percent in most years in U.S., British, and Japanese financial markets.[5] Although the government now issues long-term, inflation-indexed bonds that could be used to back inflation-protected annuities, a market has yet to emerge for such a product. Annuity purchasers seem reluctant to accept a real rate of interest of about 3.75 percent—less insurance companies' commissions, other administrative costs, and profits—which is what this protection would entail.

HOW MUCH SOCIAL ASSISTANCE?

Social Security has always provided more generous benefits, relative to earnings or past payroll tax contributions, to some participants than to others. The big gainers are low earners. For example, although $30,000 earners pay half the payroll taxes of $60,000 earners, they receive pensions that are only 29 percent smaller.

Benefits also are higher for couples and families than for single beneficiaries. Social Security provides benefits to elderly spouses equal to half of the retired worker's benefit if the spouse has had no or only a limited work history. When the retired worker dies, the surviving spouse's benefit is raised to the level of the deceased worker's benefit. If the retired worker has dependent children, Social Security also provides a benefit for them.[6] Similar benefits are provided to survivors when a worker becomes disabled or dies before reaching the retirement age.

Social Security benefits for surviving spouses and children of deceased workers and retirees comprise a kind of life insurance that is paid out in monthly installments, rather than as a lump sum. The estimated value of this life insurance for active workers in 1997 was $12 trillion. Such benefits and the benefits paid to

BOX 3–3
THE PRICE OF ANNUITIES

The annual payout that insurance companies offer 65-year-old men in return for a $100,000 annuity varies widely.[a]

	ANNUAL PAYOUT	RATE OF RETURN AS PERCENT OF YIELD ON	
		TREASURY BONDS	CORPORATE BONDS
Average company	$9,528	82	74
Ten highest-payout companies	10,464	90	82
Ten lowest-payout companies	8,700	75	68

The average annuity provides a rate of return 26 percent lower than a 65-year-old man would realize on corporate bonds if he lived exactly the average life expectancy of 65-year-old men. About 10 percentage points of this differential arises because those who buy annuities live longer than average. The remainder arises because companies selling annuities have marketing and administrative costs and must earn a profit. Because individual companies have different cost structures, have different expectations about how much they can earn on their investments, and may sell to groups with different life expectancies, there is wide variation among companies in their payout rates.

Whatever the source of the differential, two facts are clear. First, a man who purchases an annuity is giving up 18 to 32 percent of the return he could earn if he invested directly in a corporate bond fund (essentially similar conclusions apply to women). To be sure, the purchaser gets something valuable in return—the assurance that the payment will last as long as he lives. Under certain assumptions this insurance may be worth the cost charged by the *average* insurance company.

The second fact is that it pays to shop around. The top-payout companies offer 17 percent more than the bottom-payout companies. The value of insurance against outliving one's assets easily offsets the extra charges of the highest payout companies. But unless people are unusually worried about outliving their assets, most will be better off "self-insuring"—investing conservatively and spending gradually—than buying annuities from the lowest-payout companies.

a. Olivia S. Mitchell, James M. Poterba, and Mark J. Warshawsky, "New Evidence on the Money's Worth of Individual Annuities," NBER Working Paper 6002, National Bureau of Economic Research, Cambridge, Mass., April 1997.

retired workers' spouses with limited work histories clearly have more value to married than to single workers and more importance to families with children than to the childless. Nevertheless, married workers and those with large families pay the same payroll tax rate on their earnings as single workers with no spouses or children.

Taken together, these provisions reduce the likelihood that low earners, couples, and surviving spouses and dependent children will be poor. In fact, Social Security keeps twice as many people out of poverty as does all—cash and in-kind—government means-tested assistance. The fact that Social Security protects workers against low earnings as well as disability and death of a breadwinner means that the total return workers receive for their payroll taxes is higher than the financial return as measured by the actual pension benefits. People routinely pay significant sums for term life insurance or fire insurance although the benefits consumers expect to receive from such insurance are much smaller than the premiums. People buy such insurance because they prize the protection it affords from large risks they cannot afford to bear. The value of such insurance and the sense of security it provides should be added to the actual pension payments in computing the total return to Social Security.

MAKING DEFINED-CONTRIBUTION PLANS PROGRESSIVE

Defined-contribution pension plans can provide assistance to low earners and other vulnerable people in one of three ways.

Subsidies. The most direct is to subsidize the contributions of low earners. For example, the government could make supplementary payments to the retirement accounts of low earners whose mandatory contributions may be too small to support adequate pensions. Inequities would be unavoidable if subsidies were based on individual workers' earnings because some low earners do not belong to low-income households, others might have worked only part-time or for part of the year, and still others with low earnings in one year will become quite wealthy in the future. Unintended subsidies can be reduced but not without adding considerable complexity to the system. For example, the government subsidy could be means-tested or tied to the number of hours worked. Similar inappropriate subsidies arise under Social Security, but they are less troublesome because benefits are based on earnings averaged over a worker's lifetime.

Hybrid Plans. Linking a defined-contribution pension plan to a defined-benefit system can ensure a minimum level of support for low earners and provide additional support for spouses with limited work histories. For example, a defined-benefit plan could provide all retirees an inflation-protected flat benefit related to the number of years worked plus a spouse's benefit. The individual retirement accounts in the defined-contribution plan could supplement the flat benefit.[7]

Hybrid plans can be designed to achieve whatever degree of income protection society deems appropriate. The relevant question is whether such a plan could be enacted and sustained. Social Security has forged a political alliance between high and moderate earners who receive sizable pensions and low earners who receive social assistance. Splitting pensions and social assistance into separate programs would break this alliance. Over time, such a separation could weaken public support for assistance to low earners, spouses with limited work histories, and dependent family members.

Income-tested Assistance. Social assistance for survivors and the elderly poor can also come through income-tested programs that could be expanded to supplement a defined-contribution pension system. Unfortunately, income tests are costly to administer, adding as much as 10 percent to total program costs. In the United States, income-tested programs also typically carry a stigma that deters some people who are legally entitled to benefits from claiming them, a serious disadvantage in a benefit intended to be universal.

A SUMMING UP

Social Security has never been known primarily as a program to fight poverty or to provide aid to families with children. Nevertheless, it has provided extra benefits to low earners and families with children for six decades. Through these extra benefits, it has contributed significantly to the reduction of poverty among beneficiaries from these groups. Furthermore, this assistance has been provided without the use of means tests. Any shift to a defined-contribution system will make it more difficult and controversial to sustain such assistance, as it would be cumbersome to administer and vulnerable to political attack.

HOW MUCH RESERVE ACCUMULATION?

Elected officials in the United States and most other developed countries have preferred pay-as-you-go (PAYGO) financing for their pension systems for a simple reason. Building large reserves requires either that small benefits be paid for several decades after a plan's inception or that taxes be high enough to pay significant benefits *and* build reserves. Initial Social Security pensions, although modest, far exceeded what the average beneficiary's payroll tax contributions justified. For example, the group that turned 65 between 1950 and 1955 received benefits that were almost four times higher than their past contributions warranted.

Some deride pay-as-you-go financing as a Ponzi or pyramid scheme, invoking the same plan that the infamous Signor Ponzi developed in the 1920s, through which he paid high returns to early depositors using funds gathered from later depositors (see Box 3–4, page 45). When doubts about the scheme's viability arose, new deposits dried up. The scheme collapsed. Depositors cried foul. And Signor Ponzi went to jail.

Because pay-as-you-go financing operates on a similar principle—benefits are paid with funds contributed by workers whose later claims are paid by succeeding generations of workers—some suggest that pay-as-you-go Social Security is also inherently unsound. The analogy is flawed in two crucial respects: Ponzi promised larger returns than any plausible growth of his "customer base" could sustain, and his system was *voluntary*. But neither is the case with Social Security. If Social Security promised benefits that grew much faster than the nation's economy, it too would be unsustainable. But pay-as-you-go social insurance can provide a return on contributions equal to the rate of growth of total earnings—the sum of the growth of the workforce and of earnings per worker (see Box 3–5, page 46). Similarly, if Social Security were voluntary—for example, if high-income wage earners and those who felt they could do better saving privately could opt out of the system—it would soon collapse; but it is mandatory (see Box 3–6, page 47, for an explanation of why voluntary Social Security cannot work).

At present, Social Security is not run on a pay-as-you-go basis. Approximately $4 of every $5 of Social Security income now goes to pay current benefits.[8] The remaining $1 is invested in U.S. government securities. In 1998, Social Security revenues exceeded expenditures

BOX 3–4
THE COLORFUL LIFE OF CHARLES PONZI

Charles Ponzi's profession is listed in the *Biographical Almanac* as "swindler." Ponzi's name is immortal because he had the genius to turn a legitimate business venture into a very lucrative crime.

A native of Italy, Ponzi began his life of crime early, stealing from his parents and parish priests. He emigrated to Canada and then to the United States, where additional petty crimes led to short jail sentences. In 1919, he discovered "arbitrage"—making money by buying the same asset in one market and selling it at a higher price in another market. The asset was postage stamps. The International Postal Union sold certificates that could be used in post offices of various nations to purchase sufficient postage to send letters internationally. The cost of such certificates in Spain was 1 cent. The certificate was good for 5 cents worth of postage in the United States. This is the same sort of transaction in which "arbitrageurs" engage, buying grain, currency, or other materials in one market and selling it in another where prices are higher. Such transactions, which tend to raise prices in the low-price market and lower them in the high-price market, are entirely legitimate.

Ponzi had an innovation—he lied. After explaining the transaction to gullible investors, he neglected to inform them that he really had no way to convert the U.S. stamps back to cash. He also failed to tell them that he was not buying postal certificates at all. Instead, he simply kept what initial investors paid him and, as more money rolled in, he repaid the initial investors, never failing to skim funds for himself. Ponzi did very nicely, collecting "investments" worth $154 million in 1996 dollars.[a] He bought a twenty-room mansion and a bank, and in general lived very well. Eventually, he made a very serious blunder. He hired a public relations expert to help him maintain his image, an *honest* public relations expert, who quickly recognized fraud and reported it to the authorities. Ponzi ended up in prison, from which he wrote letters to former investors expressing regret that he could not help them but promising to do so as soon as he got out. The immigration authorities had other plans, however, deporting Ponzi to his native Italy. With few resources, he joined Mussolini's fascist movement and became a high ranking treasury official, until his incompetence was discovered. At that point, he was sent to Brazil as manager of the new national airline Al Italia. Following the war and Mussolini's death, Ponzi lost his job and his money. He died penniless, tended only by a nun.

Frauds that closely resemble Ponzi's scheme abound. Everyone seems susceptible. One-sixth of the citizens of Romania fell for a Ponzi scheme in 1993. Nearer to home, the celebrated Foundation for New Era Philanthropy, a scheme that promised to double and triple the gifts wealthy donors wanted to give to charity, gulled people as sophisticated as William Simon, former Treasury Department secretary; John Whitehead, former managing partner of the investment firm, Goldman, Sachs; and Laurence Rockefeller, financier.

---

a. David Segal, "Money for Nothing: Forget the Work Ethic; Mr. Ponzi Showed Us the Real American Dream," *Washington Post,* Outlook, June 2, 1996, p. 1.

Box 3–5
What Return Can
Pay-as-You-Go Social Insurance Pay?

The average real rate of return on payroll tax payments equals the growth of real earnings, which in turn equals the growth of employment multiplied by the growth of output per worker.

This is the fundamental proposition of pay-as-you-go social insurance. The following examples illustrate this proposition. Suppose that people's adult lives are divided into two periods. They work for the first period and collect pensions in the second. Assume further that N people comprise each cohort or age group. Each worker earns E. Both population and earnings are stable. The payroll tax rate is t. That means that each worker pays taxes of tE and tax collections from each cohort are tEN.

Under pay-as-you-go financing, all taxes are paid out as benefits to the N members of the older cohort. Benefits per retiree equal total tax collections, tEN, divided by the population of retirees, N, or tE per retiree. That is the same as their past payroll tax payments. With no population growth and no growth of earnings, the rate of return is also zero. Workers get back just what they paid in—no more, no less.

Now assume that each successive cohort has total earnings that are higher than the one before by some amount, say, $100Z$ percent. This growth can arise because either population or earnings-per-worker increases.

If earnings for the oldest cohort, the group that is currently retired, was EN, and the earnings of the working cohort is $(1 + Z)EN$. The retired cohort paid payroll taxes of tE per person. Its benefits, based on the payroll taxes collected from the next cohort, total $t(1 + Z)EN$. Divided among the N retirees, the benefit per retiree is $t(1 + Z)EN/N = t(1 + Z)E$. Thus the pension is $(1 + Z)$ times larger than the taxes each retiree paid, providing an economic return of Z, the same as the growth of total earnings.

This example is oversimplified in various ways. Work lives are typically longer than retirement. Growth of population and earnings per worker varies from year to year. Payroll tax rates and benefit formulas change over time. Benefits may be more generous for some workers than for others based on earnings or family circumstances. But on the average and over time, the basic proposition holds—the real rate of return under pay-as-you-go social insurance equals the growth of real earnings.

---

by about $100 billion. Reserves totaled close to $760 billion. Surpluses are projected to reach $183 billion in 2011, and total reserves are projected to reach a maximum of $3.78 trillion in 2020. These figures are impressive, but not nearly as large as they would be if the system were fully funded. Workers receive a return on their payroll taxes that is a blend of the PAYGO return, currently about 1 percent, and the yield on government securities, projected to average 2.8 percent.[9] If

---

BOX 3–6
WHY VOLUNTARY SOCIAL SECURITY CANNOT WORK

Some commentators on Social Security have urged that workers be permitted to "opt out" of the program as long as they can demonstrate that they are personally saving at least as much as they would have paid in payroll taxes. That approach, its supporters maintain, assures that workers will save, but it does not dictate the form of that saving. Any system that broadens the range of choice, it is argued, must improve individual welfare.

The argument for permitting people to save on their own is appealing—if people want to do something and it isn't illegal, why not let them do it? The answer is that even if people who opt out are correctly making self-interested decisions, their actions reduce the choices of others and are likely to lower overall welfare.

Under pay-as-you-go financing, workers pay taxes now to support current benefit payments of retirees, but claim benefits for themselves later, possibly decades later. Any person who withdraws from the system removes revenues necessary to pay current benefits *to others* and uses those revenues to accumulate reserves *for himself or herself.* If nothing else is done, revenues to sustain current benefits will be insufficient. To sustain these benefits, therefore, some other tax would have to be imposed. Most of the added burden would fall on workers who did not "opt out." Each worker who opts out is able to offload part of his or her share of the costs of supporting current retirees. If, in the end, all workers left the system but benefits for current pensioners were maintained, everyone would face higher taxes because they would collectively need to pay sufficient taxes to sustain benefits as well as make separate deposits to their own accounts.

High earners, single workers, and members of childless families are particularly likely to opt out because Social Security treats them less generously than it does low earners and members of large families. But their withdrawal would threaten the resources needed to sustain the social assistance provided by Social Security because they pay higher taxes relative to promised benefits than does the average worker. By leaving the system and placing their payroll taxes in their own accounts, high earners and members of small families who opt out would escape bearing their share of the cost to achieve these social objectives.

Finally, opting out is not practical because people's circumstances change. Workers marry, have children, get divorced, lose jobs, become disabled, and so on. Savings that seemed adequate under one set of circumstances may prove to be insufficient in other situations. Unless those who opted out had to buy insurance to protect themselves from adverse developments and were required to invest in low-risk assets, some would find themselves dependent on government charity later on. This would impose costs on those workers who did not opt out.

---

reserves were invested in assets that generated higher returns, workers would receive more pension per dollar of taxes paid. To the extent that the benefit formula promises to provide workers a higher return on their taxes than this blended rate, future contributions will have to be raised or benefits lowered.

TO ACCUMULATE OR NOT TO ACCUMULATE?

A lot of ink has been spilled in intellectually interesting debates over whether Social Security initially should have been financed on a pay-as-you-go basis, or reserves should have been accumulated. As a practical matter, this debate is pointless. The decision of elected officials in the late 1930s and 1940s to pay relatively generous retirement benefits to retirees whose working careers had been blighted by the Great Depression cannot be undone.[10]

The question now is whether to build reserves in the future, and if so, how to build them—within the Social Security system or through some alternative defined-contribution pension structure. There is no costless or politically painless way to build reserves. Someone has to pay for them, through either reduced benefits or increased taxes.[11] Cutting benefits would renege, at least in part, on promises to retirees and older workers and impose hardship on some.

If taxes are increased—now or in the future—active workers will have to support pensions not only for current beneficiaries but also to save for their own reserve accumulation. To avoid this choice, some have suggested that payroll taxes should go into the personal retirement accounts of young workers and bonds be issued to pay pensions of retirees and older workers. However, building individual accounts by issuing government bonds is a financial shell game. Issuing bonds creates no new assets and adds nothing to national saving or productive capacity. The assets in workers' accounts would be exactly matched by new liabilities of the federal government. The real economic benefits come from increased saving, which requires either tax increases or benefit cuts to force workers or beneficiaries to reduce their consumption.

The benefit cuts or tax increases necessary to build reserves are the same whether they occur within a defined-benefit program or within a defined-contribution program. Furthermore, the economic effects do not depend on whether Social Security is retained or replaced by private individual accounts (see Box 3–7). In either case, raising reserves by $1 billion boosts national saving by $1 billion. Individuals may offset part or all of the intended saving by saving less in other forms. Similarly, reserves in Social Security may cause elected officials to raise spending or cut taxes elsewhere in the government budget.[12]

BOX 3–7
WHAT HAPPENS WHEN WE SAVE $1 BILLION?

PRIVATE SAVING

Private savers save	+ $1 billion
Private saving available for private investment	+ $1 billion
U.S.-owned capital stock grows	+ $1 billion

ADDITION TO SOCIAL SECURITY RESERVES

Social security reserves rise	+ $1 billion
Social security trustees buy additional government bonds	+ $1 billion
Government sells fewer bonds to private sector	- $1 billion
Private saving available for private investment rises	+ $1 billion
U.S.-owned capital stock grows	+ $1 billion

In either case, the return equals $1 billion multiplied by the private rate of return.

However reserves are created, the central questions remain: Is the bill worth paying? If so, what is the best way to pay it? The debate on these issues are arcane and technical, and so we present only a few of the arguments that protagonists raise.

The Case against Reserve Accumulation. Opponents of reserve accumulation start by noting that future generations will, almost certainly, be richer than we are. Forcing us to save more reduces our consumption to make our wealthier children and grandchildren richer still. Nothing is stopping us, it is argued, from saving more as individuals if we want to help out our heirs. But why should we be forced to do so collectively? Shouldn't this be a matter of individual choice?

Even if more saving is desirable, policies to force saving might not work. If public pensions build reserves and benefits become more secure, people might save less individually or through their company pension plans, or they might borrow more. When the economic dust has settled, total saving may be little changed. It could just take different forms—larger public pension surpluses and less personal net saving. Even if more saving is desirable and saving could be increased by raising pension-related taxes, levies other than the payroll tax may be fairer and more conducive to economic efficiency. Furthermore, if taxes are to be increased, there may be better things to do with those resources than enriching future generations. Fighting poverty, providing health care to the uninsured, improving educational opportunities, cleaning up the environment, combating crime, and investing in medical research and public infrastructure rank higher than boosting national saving in the judgment of some observers. Many of these activities could improve the lives of both current and future generations.

The Case for Reserve Accumulation. Despite these concerns, we believe that the case for measures to boost national saving is persuasive. Evidence suggests that the lure of current consumption overwhelms prudent planning for future wants so that people consistently save too little for their own good. Furthermore, income taxes or failings of financial markets deny people the full economic returns from saving, and thereby discourage saving. Still others believe that Social Security, Medicare, and other forms of assistance blunt personal incentives to save. Since these programs build reserves smaller than those individuals would have to accumulate to provide themselves equivalent protection, they depress saving.[13]

Finally, many observers doubt that the myriad discrete decisions of individuals and businesses necessarily produce exactly the right amount of saving. They point to two troublesome facts. First, Americans' saving is low. Americans now save only about half as much, measured as a share of total output, as they did during the quarter-century after World War II. And they save a lower portion of their output than do citizens of other major industrial nations. Second, the baby boomers are aging. They will soon begin to retire and become dependent on active workers for pensions and health care. Boosting saving, investment, and productivity in anticipation of that event will raise output per worker and relieve future workers of some or all of the burden of supporting the aging baby boomers. So much has been said about the looming costs of the baby boomers— including a great deal that is quite misleading—that we shall devote all of Chapter 4 to this issue.

CONCLUSION

However one comes down on the desirability of boosting saving, the debate about Social Security reform has to face two other core issues. The first concerns how the inescapable risks associated with any pension system should be distributed. This issue shows up as a technical debate over whether the nation's basic mandatory retirement system should be a defined-benefit (DB) pension system or a defined-contribution (DC) pension system. As one wag has put it, "DB or not DB, that is the question."

We conclude that the strengths and advantages of a defined-benefit system outweigh those of a defined-contribution system *for the program that is intended to assure basic income during retirement, disability, and survivorship*. Risks in such a program should be broadly shared by society—by high earners and low earners, by big families and small families, by retirees and current and future workers.

The chief argument for imposing these risks on individuals is the claim that individuals will make better saving and investment decisions if they bear these risks themselves than if the risks are diffused more broadly. For most personal financial decisions, the argument for personal responsibility is persuasive. The financial system of the United States depends on risk bearing and provides financial rewards to individuals who bear risk. But the argument that individuals should bear risks carries little weight in the case of the basic pension program. First, individuals are ill-equipped to handle the investment, inflation, longevity, and other risks they would have to shoulder under a defined-contribution pension system. The prime justification for a mandatory pension system is the recognition that many people will *not* make good decisions about how much to save, how to invest what they have saved, and how rapidly to spend their retirement savings. Many will save too little and end their careers unable to support themselves adequately during retirement or disability. Some will invest too conservatively, in very safe but low-yielding assets that will not grow fast enough to sustain an adequate pension. Some will choose investments that turn out poorly. Most are likely to shun annuities and be exposed to longevity risk. If the experience to date with individual accounts in the United Kingdom is any guide, administrative costs will be high and few will protect their basic pension from inflation by purchasing the inflation-indexed securities now issued by the Treasury Department.[14]

Rather than exposing workers individually to these risks, it would be far better, we believe, to spread them among active and future workers and current beneficiaries. That is precisely what a defined-benefit plan does and what a defined-contribution plan does not do. For these reasons, the defined-benefit character of the Social Security system should be preserved.

A mandatory defined-contribution system could require that contributions be invested in a balanced mix of indexed mutual funds (stocks and bonds, domestic and foreign). Rules could require that all retirees use their accumulated assets to purchase inflation-indexed annuities of at least a minimum value, annuities that covered both workers and their spouses. Nevertheless, such a system would not provide protection from broad swings in market values that might leave some cohorts much worse off than others.

Nor would it address the second core issue involved in the current debate over the future of the nation's basic pension program, namely, how to provide for the program's social objectives. It is important, we believe, to ensure adequate benefits for low-wage workers and to provide extra benefits for spouses and children of deceased and disabled workers. It is important also to supply some additional support to spouses who have not participated fully in the paid labor force, often because they have devoted much of their time to rearing children or performing unpaid services in schools, churches, hospitals, and other voluntary organizations. Almost all participants in the Social Security reform debate acknowledge the importance of sustaining assistance to support these social functions, as our review of reform plans in Chapter 7 indicates. They do so because they understand that income inequality has risen rapidly, that real earnings of unskilled and semiskilled workers have actually been falling, and that poverty is a significant problem among the disabled and older surviving spouses of deceased workers. We shall return to this issue when we evaluate the various proposals for Social Security reform.

4

WILL THE BABY BOOMERS
BREAK THE BANK?

The 77 million baby boomers, born from 1946 through 1964, are marching toward retirement! Between 2008 and 2026, the fraction of the population age 62 and over and eligible for Social Security retirement benefits will increase from 15.7 percent to 22.8 percent. Unless birth rates rise sharply and unexpectedly, the elderly will form a permanently larger share of the population. How much will the baby boomers' retirement cost? Will these costs cut into the living standards of active workers if nothing is done to reduce currently promised benefits?

THE BURDEN OF SOCIAL SECURITY:
PAST, PRESENT, AND FUTURE

The most widely cited indicator of the burden that Social Security places on the rest of society is the ratio of beneficiaries to workers.[1] Active workers must produce the food, clothing, shelter, health care, and other goods and services for themselves and their families, for Social Security beneficiaries, and for other members of the population who are not working. The higher the ratio of beneficiaries to workers, the smaller the proportion of total production economically inactive members of the population, including Social Security beneficiaries, consume.

BENEFICIARIES AND WORKERS

In 1998, there were thirty Social Security beneficiaries for every hundred workers. By 2031, when all the baby boomers will have reached the age at which unreduced Social Security benefits will be paid, projections indicate that there will be fifty beneficiaries for every hundred workers, an increase of two-thirds. This trend, although striking, is neither new nor unexpected. For the past two decades, the government's official demographic projections have painted this same picture. In other words, none of the projected long-term deficit that has emerged since 1983, when Congress last enacted major changes in the Social Security system, can be attributed to unforeseen demographic developments. The projected long-term deficit that has emerged since then is attributable to changed economic assumptions and revised methods of estimating the program's long-run costs and revenues.[2]

Looking back over six decades of Social Security history, the changing ratio of Social Security beneficiaries to workers tells a complicated story. In the early years of Social Security few people over age 65 received benefits. Most had stopped working before the system began or had been employed in one of the many jobs that were initially uncovered by Social Security. In 1945, five years after benefits were first paid, there were only two beneficiaries per hundred workers. Since then, the ratio of beneficiaries to workers has risen gradually as the proportion of 65-year-olds eligible for benefits has increased. In 1950, when only 16 percent of those 65 and older received benefits, there were six beneficiaries per hundred workers. It was not until 1958, when there were seventeen beneficiaries for every hundred workers, that over half of the elderly were receiving Social Security benefits.

Until recently, two developments helped to hold down the ratio of beneficiaries to covered workers. First, between 1946 and 1983, Congress gradually extended Social Security to domestic and agricultural workers, the self-employed, employees of nonprofit organizations, federal employees, members of the armed services, and most state and local workers—the 45 percent of the labor force initially excluded from coverage. Today, 96 percent of all civilian workers hold jobs covered by Social Security, and most of the remaining 4 percent will work in covered employment at some point in their lives and become eligible for benefits. Second, the labor force expanded rapidly as baby boomers grew up and went to work and as women increasingly took paid jobs. The influx of women more than offset a drop in male labor force participation.

A third factor—the rapid growth of worker productivity and earnings—held down benefit costs as a percent of payroll until the mid-1970s. The slowdown in growth of earnings and payroll tax revenues that started then and is projected to continue means that higher payroll tax rates will be needed to sustain any level of future benefits.

THE REST OF THE BURDEN STORY

Active members of the labor force have to support *all* economically inactive members of the population—children and nonaged adults who are not employed for pay, as well as Social Security beneficiaries. As it happens, the proportion of the population consisting of children and nonaged adults who are not working for pay has fallen over the past three decades and is projected to fall further in the future. Consequently, the number of people each worker will support is projected to rise only modestly—approximately 6 percent—between now and 2040, even though the number of elderly will soar (see Figure 4–1, page 58). The number of economically inactive members of the population per hundred workers was much higher in the past (156 in 1960) than it was in the mid-1990s (103 in 1995) or than it is projected to be in the future (115 in 2040).

NOT ALL DEPENDENTS ARE ALIKE

The increase in the number of mouths that active workers will have to feed is too small to attract much notice. But this way of looking at the problems created by population changes is oversimplified. First, the government pays directly for a larger share of the cost of supporting the elderly and disabled than of the cost of supporting children and economically inactive nonaged adults. While workers

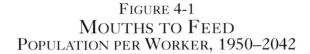

FIGURE 4-1
MOUTHS TO FEED
POPULATION PER WORKER, 1950–2042

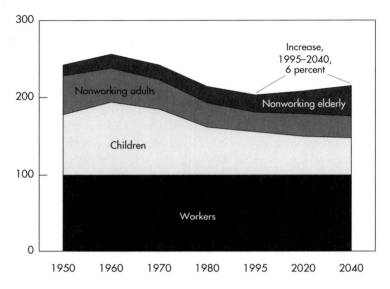

Source: National Academy of Social Insurance, "How Many People Does Each Worker Support?" *Social Insurance Update* 2, issue 4, April 1997.

eventually bear all these costs, as the government is only their agent, families *directly* bear primary responsibility for feeding, clothing, housing, and providing medical care for children and most nonretired adults. They receive help from state and local governments, which finance education, and from federal and state governments, which jointly provide income assistance, food vouchers, and health care subsidies for many low-income children and adults. As the composition of the dependent population shifts from children and able-bodied nonaged adults to retirees and the disabled, direct economic burdens on families will decline, while the costs to government of paying for the health and pension benefits of the elderly will rise.

Simply counting heads is misleading also because the average aged or disabled person costs more to support than the average child. Children and their nonworking caretakers live in families that enjoy the economies of scale available to multiperson households. A greater portion of the elderly and disabled, on the other hand, live alone or in two-person households. While children generate costs for publicly supported education, the average child consumes only about one-third as much health care as the average elderly person does.[3] On balance, projected changes in the *composition* of the dependent population will increase overall economic burdens.

THE BURDEN IN ECONOMIC TERMS

Just how large is the current burden of supporting the elderly and disabled, and how much will it grow as the baby boomers retire? In 1998, the benefit and administrative costs of Social Security amounted to 4.6 percent of GDP, about one-third more than defense expenditures and roughly the same as personal consumption spending on the purchase and operation of automobiles. By 2040, Social Security is projected to cost 6.8 percent of GDP, an increase of 2.2 percentage points in four decades. This increase is comparable to the 2 percent of GDP growth in cost of Social Security that took place between 1970 and 1982, a period less than a third as long as the 1998 to 2040 interval. It is also less than one-third of the growth of defense spending as a share of GDP—7.3 percentage points—that occurred between 1948 and 1955 when the Cold War intensified. It is slightly more than the 2.1 percentage points of GDP increase in federal spending on Medicare and Medicaid between 1980 and 1997. These increases were large but did not cause political crises or significant economic dislocation.

But Social Security is far from the whole story when it comes to the burden that retirement of baby boomers will impose on society. Between 1998 and 2040, Medicare spending is projected to increase by 3.6 percentage points of GDP. Medicaid spending, roughly two-thirds of which provides health services to low-income elderly and disabled persons, is projected to increase by about 2.4 percentage points of GDP over the next four decades. In addition, the costs of Supplementary Security Income (SSI) and food stamp benefits for the low-income aged and disabled may also rise. Finally, private expenditures on long-term care will also grow.

The projected increase in the cost of Social Security alone, or in combination with Medicare and the other programs, is significant but is not likely to overwhelm future economic growth. If real per capita income grows 1.2 percent annually—a bit slower than the rate at which per capita output has risen over the 1990s—real GDP per person will rise 65 percent by 2040.[4] Of this amount, just under one-third would be needed to deal with the projected increase in the cost of Social Security and Medicare assuming *nothing* is done to curb the growth of spending on these programs. Thus, moderate economic growth would enable future workers both to enjoy rising living standards and to pay the added taxes necessary to sustain currently projected benefit costs. The decision to levy higher taxes would, however, still be difficult and divisive.

What Can We Do About It?

Americans can act now to lighten the burden on future workers of supporting the baby boomers in two ways. Congress can scale back benefits payable in the future to retirees, the disabled, and survivors. Or Americans can adopt policies to increase economic growth. In Chapter 6 we examine a package of measures to restore balance to Social Security that includes a number of reductions in future benefits. Here we review two possible ways to boost economic growth—expanding the total number of workers and making each worker more productive.

Enlarging the Workforce

Faster population growth eventually enlarges the labor force and the economy's productive capacity. Unfortunately, few effective and politically acceptable ways exist to raise population growth. Current fertility rates will just about sustain an unchanged population. They are not projected to increase, and there is little evidence that acceptable public policy initiatives can do much to raise them. Furthermore, decades must pass before additional children that a pronatalist policy might cause to be born could be educated, reach adulthood, enter the labor force in significant numbers, and affect national production. Increased immigration could boost the labor force rapidly. But the roughly 1 million immigrants entering the United States annually are already producing economic and social strains.

Within the limits set by the adult population, the labor force can grow only if more adults choose to work for pay. The scope for such increase is limited, however, because the proportion of adults working for pay is already at a historic high. Sixty percent of women now work for pay outside the home, up from 38 percent in 1960, and Social Security's long-run projections assume that an even higher fraction of women will enter the paid labor force in the future. Large additional increases are unlikely.

The story for nonaged men is rather different. As women have moved into the paid labor force, men—especially those age 50 to 65—have moved out, largely through earlier retirement. The proportion of 65-year-old men in the paid labor force has dropped from 77 percent in 1940 to 36 percent in the mid-1990s (Figure 4–2). This trend reflects the fundamental economic fact that as people grow richer they want to have more leisure, which they get through shorter work weeks, longer vacations, and earlier retirement.

FIGURE 4–2
MALE LABOR FORCE PARTICIPATION RATES
VARIOUS YEARS, 1910–96

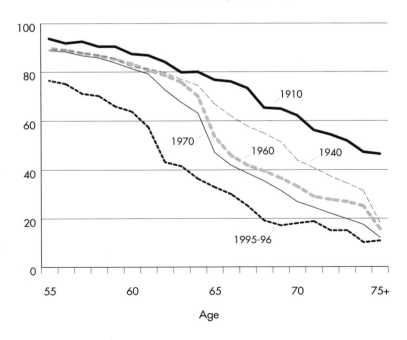

Age

Source: Unpublished figure prepared by Gary Burtless, The Brookings Institution.

Social Security and private pensions have made earlier retirement possible for workers who have little personal savings. In fact, private pensions in the past expressly encouraged retirement of older and more highly compensated workers. To achieve this result, pensions for workers rose little or not at all after they reached a certain age. Social Security, in contrast, is roughly neutral with respect to retirement for workers up to age 65 because pensions for those who continue to work past age 61 are increased approximately enough to compensate for the foregone pensions.[5]

After dropping for decades, labor force participation rates of older males have been steady since the late 1980s. It is unclear whether the trend toward ever-earlier retirement has stopped permanently or has merely paused in response to an unusually strong economy, as happened during the boom years of the 1960s. Furthermore, policy changes have made it easier for older workers to remain in the labor force. Bans on discrimination against older workers were enacted in 1967 and 1990. Employer-imposed mandatory retirement rules were prohibited in 1986. Businesses are now required to continue pension contributions on behalf of those who work past the normal retirement age. In addition, the increment in Social Security benefits for those who work past age 65 was raised. We will not know for several years whether men have decided to work longer or are just adjusting to a new policy environment and taking advantage of the strong economy. If men could be encouraged to work even a bit longer, the effect on the labor force could be significant. For example, if men age 55 and older could be encouraged to work at the same rates as they did in 1970, the labor force would be enlarged by 2.9 million, which is one-fifth of the total projected labor force growth over the next decade.

The most obvious ways to encourage later retirement involve changing Social Security. Benefits could be cut either across the board, or just for early retirees, to encourage older workers to remain in the labor force. The age of initial entitlement could be raised. The retirement test—the reduction in benefits imposed when earnings exceed specified thresholds—could be liberalized. Or the delayed retirement credit—the increase in future benefits provided to compensate those whose benefits are cut because of the earnings test—could be increased.

Raising the "Normal" Retirement Age. The age at which unreduced retirement benefits are paid—the so-called normal retirement age—is now 65, as it has been since 1940 when benefits were first paid. In 1983, Congress approved legislation that will increase this age to 67 over the 2000 to 2022 period.[6] Many people refer to this change as an increase in the retirement age, but that designation is misleading because the change in law lowers benefits proportionally for all ages and does not increase the age of initial entitlement. Deeper benefit cuts brought about by further increases in the age at which unreduced benefits are paid might cause some older workers to defer retirement, although empirical estimates indicate that the effects would be small.

Early Retirement Benefits. The availability of Social Security benefits at age 62 facilitates early retirement, even if it does not penalize continued work. Approximately 25 percent of men still working retire at age 62, a larger proportion than at any other age. However, claiming benefits before age 65 permanently lowers benefits not only for the worker but also for the surviving spouse. A larger early-retirement penalty might cause some people to continue working but would not affect benefits for those who worked until the age at which unreduced benefits are paid. Unfortunately, it could also increase poverty among survivors of workers who retired early anyway. Already, 23 percent of women age 65 and older who live alone are poor, and just under half have incomes below 150 percent of the poverty threshold.

Age of Initial Entitlement. Neither of the two previous benefit cuts would alter the age at which benefits are first available. Although life expectancy at age 62 has increased by 3.6 years since 1961 when men first became eligible for early retirement benefits, raising the age of initial entitlement has not been politically popular. Some workers develop physical and mental limitations or are employed in strenuous jobs that make work past age 61 increasingly onerous. In addition, raising the age of initial entitlement saves little money in the long run because the increase in benefits associated with delaying retirement from age 62 to age 65 approximately offsets the shorter period over which benefits must be paid. Raising the age of initial entitlement from 62 to 63 or 64 might well encourage continued work, however. Unlike the two previous benefit cuts, it would not risk permanently lowering benefits for surviving spouses.

The Delayed Retirement Credit. In addition to raising the age at which unreduced benefits are paid, Congress in 1983 also liberalized the "delayed retirement credit"—the increase in benefits paid to those who work past the age at which unreduced benefits are paid and to those who earn enough to have their benefits reduced by the earnings test. When this change is fully phased in for those reaching age 62 in 2005, the increase will approximately compensate an average worker for the value of benefits lost because of the retirement test. In other words, the lifetime value of benefits the average worker can expect to receive will be independent of when that worker chooses to retire. Raising the delayed retirement credit still more—in effect, providing increases in lifetime benefits for later retirement—could further encourage later retirement but not without increasing program costs.

The Retirement Test. Because Social Security is intended to replace lost earnings, it has paid benefits only when the earnings of those age 62 and older are below specified thresholds. This "retirement test" has been remarkably unpopular. Many members of Congress regard the restriction as unfair and think that it has discouraged work by older men and women. Consequently, Congress has steadily raised the amounts people can earn without loss of benefits. In 1999, the retirement test for those age 65 to 69 will reduce benefits $1 for every $3 of earnings in excess of $15,500; the allowable earnings threshold will rise gradually to $30,000 by 2002. For those age 62 to 64, benefits will be reduced $1 for every $2 of earnings above $9,360, a threshold that will rise to $10,440 in 2002.[7]

Relaxing or repealing the retirement test might boost labor force participation of older workers, even though the adjustments made to the future pensions of those affected by the retirement test are analytically equivalent to repealing this test. In other words, workers with average life expectancies will receive the same total lifetime benefits whether they retire at age 62 or continue working and have their benefits reduced because their earnings exceed the retirement test thresholds. However, workers may respond less to a fair delayed retirement credit than they would to higher thresholds or a repeal of the earnings test, which would let more retirees receive pensions while continuing to work.[8] Relaxation or repeal of the retirement test would have the unintended side effect of strengthening arguments for income testing of benefits, as Social Security pensions would be paid to some people who were also taking home very high salaries, in contradiction to the traditional goal of the system to "replace lost earnings."[9] In addition, they would boost government spending in the short run.

While changes in the retirement test and delayed retirement credit are unlikely to increase work by older workers very much, delaying the availability of retirement benefits beyond age 62 would discourage retirement of people who lack the liquid assets to do so. This change in benefit structure is the one most likely to boost labor supply of older Americans.

BOOSTING THE GROWTH OF OUTPUT PER WORKER

Increasing output per worker will lighten the burden of supporting a growing aged population. How fast output per worker grows depends on changes in the skills of workers, on the quantity and quality of capital that workers use, and on managerial skill and business organization.

Skills. Improved education and on-the-job training, which increase worker productivity and earnings, are desirable for reasons that have nothing to do with Social Security, but they also can help the nation meet pension costs by raising payroll tax collections. Neither individuals nor businesses normally take this connection into account when deciding how much education or training is optimal. As important as education and training may be to economic growth, public policy in this area will continue to be driven more by the desire to expand individual opportunity than by any notion that a more skilled workforce could ease the societal burden of supporting an expanding population of retirees. Nevertheless, measures to improve the quality of education and to increase the number of young people graduating from high schools, colleges, and training programs do help ease pension costs. The benefits are very slow in coming, however, because most of the labor force for the next several decades will have completed its formal education before any improvement could occur.

Technology, Managerial Skills, and Capital. Technological advance, investment, improved management, and better business organization all boost economic growth. Public policy can promote technological advance by supporting basic and applied research and by education. Competitive and open markets, judicious and limited regulation, and a tax system that distorts investment decisions as little as possible also facilitate managerial and technological innovation, which, in turn, favors rapid economic advance.

How the nation's basic pension system is financed affects national saving, which, along with net investment by foreigners, determines the growth of the nation's capital stock. Private saving by U.S. households and businesses declined sharply and surprisingly during the 1980s and 1990s. It reached a post-World War II low of 3.8 percent of disposable personal income in 1997. As the baby boomers moved into their prime earning years in the late 1980s and 1990s and their children began to leave home, retirement saving should have risen, not fallen. Reduced tax rates and new tax-sheltered savings accounts should have amplified this trend. The fact that private saving fell is both puzzling and troubling.

The recent history of government saving is quite different and more heartening. Before the mid-1970s, combined revenues of federal, state, and local governments exceeded their spending, which meant they added to national saving. For two decades starting in the mid-1970s, mushrooming federal deficits swamped the surpluses of states and localities. The government sector as a whole became a net borrower, absorbing private saving available for investment. However, the unified federal budget has moved from a deficit of 4.7 percent of GDP in 1992 to a surplus of 0.8 percent of GDP in 1998, thereby raising national saving by over 5 percent of GDP. Official budget projections suggest that the federal surpluses should gradually rise to between 1.9 and 2.6 percent of GDP by 2008, if Congress and the president can resist the temptation to use the surpluses to cut taxes and boost spending. Surpluses should continue for almost two decades, after which rising Social Security and Medicare spending for aging baby boomers will require higher taxes, spending cuts, or both to sustain surpluses.

Budget surpluses are hard to sustain because the benefits of fiscal frugality are deferred and widely diffused, while tax cuts and program expansions produce immediate and identifiable benefits for particular groups. Nevertheless, preserving the surpluses is the most reliable way to boost economic growth and help offset the added costs of supporting the baby boomers in retirement.

CONCLUSION: POLITICS VERSUS ECONOMICS

One can hardly turn on a television or open a newspaper or magazine without encountering overwrought rhetoric bewailing the insupportable burden that the baby boomers will impose on thinned ranks of future workers. From an economic standpoint, this rhetoric is detached from reality. While there is no way to eliminate the *overall economic costs* of an aging population, sweeping structural changes are not needed to close the projected long-term deficit in Social Security if the nation enjoys normal economic growth. Measures to promote economic growth, which are desirable for many reasons, would lighten the economic burden for future workers.

The political problems of meeting the costs of population aging are more substantial, however. Whether the United States is merely as rich as it is today or even richer, it will still be necessary to shift more of what the economy produces from workers to the elderly and disabled and to survivors of deceased workers. These transfers will require increased taxes if currently promised benefits remain unchanged and the method of financing Social Security is not altered. The simplest way to reduce such tax increases is to invest Social Security's reserves in assets that generate higher yields than the current portfolio of Treasury securities. Replacing Social Security with mandatory private saving in personal accounts would in no way reduce the burden. We shall examine in Chapter 5 various proposals to make this shift to the private sector and in Chapter 6 how to restore balance in Social Security.

5

PRIVATIZATION

As the twentieth century comes to a close, private enterprises operating in a competitive market stand triumphant around the world. Free markets have proven themselves the most efficient way to produce and distribute almost all goods and services. In virtually all countries, state-run monopolies and nationalized industries have been marked by inefficiency, high costs, shoddy quality, and a lack of innovation. Against this backdrop, almost any call to convert to private management a government activity that the private sector has successfully performed should command a serious and sympathetic hearing. Since many elements of Social Security, such as pension management and insurance, resemble services that the private sector delivers successfully, the strengths and weaknesses of privatizing Social Security are well worth examining.

Other than a few hardcore "libertarians"—who believe that government should make no laws restricting individual behavior and should impose no taxes other than those necessary to provide for national defense and ensure public safety—almost no one favors complete privatization of pension saving and disability and survivor's insurance. Such a step would involve not only repealing Social Security but also abandoning the notion that government should require people to save for their retirement. Most people recognize that without some requirements or powerful incentives, many of us would save too little to prepare adequately for retirement and carry too little disability and life insurance. Accordingly, virtually all who favor privatization of Social Security—"privatizers" for short—acknowledge the need for measures to compel or encourage people to save for old age and protect against the risks that they or a principal earner will become disabled or die, leaving their families with inadequate means of support.

WHAT IS PRIVATIZATION?

Privatizing Social Security entails two fundamental steps: first, establishing a defined-contribution pension system with individually owned personal retirement accounts, and second, gradually scaling back or eliminating current Social Security retirement benefits. Contributions to personal retirement accounts, like the payroll tax payments made to support Social Security, would be mandatory. Instead of supporting defined-benefit pensions for current and future workers, these payments would be deposited in individually owned, defined-contribution accounts. The funds in these accounts would be managed by private financial institutions selected by either individuals or the government. The total balances in these accounts—the contributions plus the investment returns—would be available to support a pension for the account's owner.

The balance in each worker's account would depend on how much was contributed, the account's investment returns, and administrative costs. Workers who made identical contributions throughout their working years but invested in different assets or were charged different administrative fees could end up with very different balances when they retired. Similarly, workers who invested in the same assets managed by the same financial institution could end up with very different pensions if some retired when asset prices were high and others when asset prices were low.

Privatization plans differ in several key areas: how much of Social Security the personal accounts would replace; what rules would govern investments; how benefits would be distributed; and how the transition to the new system would be handled.

SCOPE AND DISTRIBUTION

Some privatization plans would scale back Social Security and supplement these reduced benefits with pensions financed from mandatory saving in personal retirement accounts. Other plans would replace the entire old-age insurance benefit with a new defined-contribution system. Almost all privatization plans retain the disability and survivor's insurance programs, which account for about 30 percent of the total cost of Social Security, although most cut these programs' benefits. Balances in defined-contribution accounts would usually be insufficient to provide adequate survivor's or disability benefits for workers who died or became disabled in their 30s, 40s, or even 50s. Privatization plans could require that workers buy private life and disability insurance policies of a certain minimum size. However, supplementary assistance would be necessary for low earners and large families if the social assistance functions of Social Security were to be sustained. In the end, private disability and survivors programs that contained regulations to ensure that insurance carriers did not discriminate against workers with high risks would probably look very much like the current government programs, but without the administrative efficiencies of a centrally managed program.

Most, but not all, privatization plans would provide larger retirement benefits in relation to earnings and contributions to low earners than to high earners. Some would do this by retaining a scaled-back Social Security program. Others would create a new flat benefit to accompany the defined-contribution pension system. And one would supplement the contributions of low earners to the defined-contribution plan.

INVESTMENT RULES

Some privatization plans would be individually managed. They would permit workers to invest their retirement accounts in any approved financial asset, much as owners of existing Individual Retirement Accounts (IRAs) now can do. Others would permit investments only through financial organizations that were government certified through yet-to-be-specified procedures. Still other plans would be government managed. They would limit investments to a few publicly managed stock, bond, or money market index funds, similar to those currently available to federal employees under the Thrift Savings Plan (TSP). Restrictions curtail individual control over their accounts, but reduce the likelihood that the returns of some participants fall far short of broad market rates of return.

POSTRETIREMENT REGULATION

Under some plans individuals could do what they want with their account balances once they retire—withdraw funds gradually or all at once, buy an annuity, or hold their funds for their heirs. To prevent retirees from squandering their savings, becoming impoverished, and ending up on welfare, other plans would require retirees to make phased withdrawals over a number of years or buy an annuity with all or part of the retirement account balances.

TRANSITION

The transition from Social Security to a privatized system would create a knotty financial problem. Under current arrangements, most payroll taxes support pensions for *previous* generations of workers who are now retired. Under a privatized system, workers would contribute to *their own* personal retirement accounts. However, unless contributions were increased sharply, it would take a full working life to build a fund sufficient, on the average, to provide an adequate pension. Consequently, a new defined-contribution system could fully replace current Social Security benefits only for younger workers— say, those under about age 35. Since current retirees and workers over the age of 50 or 55 would have little or no accumulation in private accounts, most privatization plans continue to rely entirely on the current Social Security system for these age groups. Workers of intermediate age would receive benefits partly under the new system and partly under the old.

With all or a portion of the contributions of current workers going to personal retirement accounts, extra revenues would be needed to pay for the benefits of current retirees and those older workers still under the current system. Some privatization plans permanently or temporarily raise payroll taxes. One would redirect payroll taxes to individual accounts and pay for Social Security benefits with a new 10 percent national sales tax that would grad-ually phase out as the benefit promises for current retirees and older workers were fulfilled.

Supporters of privatization realize that it is difficult to win sup-port for a new policy if workers think they will have to pay signifi-cantly higher taxes. Accordingly, some plans have developed ways to soften the blow. One such solution is to impose a tax sufficient to cover the transition costs averaged over many years. The revenue generated by such a tax would not cover the initial costs of benefits for workers retired under the old system, and the government would have to borrow to meet the shortfall. Later on, when retirees would need smaller and smaller supplements to their growing individual accounts, the revenue from the new tax would be more than is need-ed to pay benefits to retirees still under the old or hybrid systems. The excess would be used to retire the debt issued during the early years of the transition. While borrowing reduces the additional taxes that have to be paid in the early years, higher taxes must be imposed for more years to cover interest on the early loans and eventually to pay them off.

When projections of significant and sustained budget surpluses first appeared in mid-1998, some advocates of privatization devel-oped plans that tapped these surpluses to pay for transition costs. This use of the surpluses would preclude devoting them to debt reduc-tion, tax cuts, or spending increases.

However it is handled, the transition to a privatized system would take a long time. Exactly how long depends on whether taxes are increased immediately to cover the full annual costs of Social Security benefits or borrowed funds are used to cover part of the early transition costs. If all workers age 55 or older remained entire-ly under the current system, Social Security benefits would be undi-minished for at least seven years—that is, until the first workers who would receive a portion of their benefits under the new system reached age 62. If every worker under age 30 had to rely solely on the new privatized system, the transition would not be complete until the last person who is now over age 30, and that person's spouse, died. Even after twenty-five years, the transition period would be less than half complete.

If funds are borrowed, the transition will take even longer. One plan would raise the payroll tax by 1.52 percentage points—far less than necessary to maintain Social Security for retirees and older workers while building up private account balances. To fill in the gap, this plan would require the government to borrow approximately $2 trillion (in 1998 dollars) over the first thirty-four years of the plan. The payroll tax increase would remain in force approximately seventy years to pay off the loan. This "transition" tax would last nearly as long as the modern personal income tax, which was first imposed in 1913, has been in place.

A decision to privatize Social Security would mean that, for several decades, workers would have to pay not only to build up personal account balances, but also to support pensions for older workers and retirees who were not part of the new system. This consequence is unavoidable because Social Security has an "unfunded liability"—the excess of benefit obligations to retirees and current workers over accumulated reserves. It will be necessary to pay this unfunded liability whether Social Security is privatized or the current system is retained, as we recommend in Chapter 6.[1]

ADVANTAGES OF PRIVATIZATION

Advocates of privatization claim benefits both for individuals and for society. Since plans differ, so do the advantages claimed for them. We gloss over some of these differences to facilitate consideration of the advantages of the privatization approach in general, but it is important to keep in mind that some forms of privatization are demonstrably superior to others.[2]

INCREASED RETIREMENT INCOMES

The primary attraction of privatization to individuals is the claim that it would significantly increase retirement incomes. Privatizers point out that annual real returns on investments in common stocks have averaged 8.2 percent over the *past* forty years and 11.4 percent over the past twenty years, far in excess of the projected returns on Social Security over the *next* thirty-five years of only about 1 percent.[3]

These comparisons are misleading for three reasons. First, most Social Security contributions are devoted to paying benefits to current retirees rather than to building investable balances. Workers, or tax-payers more generally, would have to meet these obligations under a privatized system just as they now must do. These payments generate no return for taxpayers, dragging down the overall yield. Second, abstracting from the contributions needed to meet current benefit obligations, the higher yield on additional funds invested in individual accounts has nothing to do with privatization. Rather, it arises from the requirement that Social Security reserves be invested in relatively low-yielding government securities. If Social Security reserves were invested in assets similar to those used to estimate the returns on personal retirement accounts, the average returns of Social Security and a privatized system would be similar. Third, one should include differences in administrative costs, which we examine later in this chapter.

INDIVIDUAL CONTROL AND SELF-RELIANCE

Most people like to have a hand in making important decisions that personally affect them, reflecting the American emphasis on self-reliance, individual freedom, and responsibility. Privatization clearly would represent a move to empower individuals.

From its earliest days, critics worried that Social Security would undermine self-reliance by protecting people from the full consequences of imprudence. Others simply deplored government interference in an activity—saving and insuring to provide protection against income loss—that they believed individuals could and should perform for themselves. Few now argue that Social Security has caused moral decay, but many believe that it has reduced personal saving.

Supporters of privatization claim that people should exercise increased control over and responsibility for their well-being during retirement. Millions already manage investments made through their company-sponsored, defined-contribution retirement plans. Everyone has complete discretion about how much to save voluntarily and how to invest it. Supporters of privatization think it is now appropriate for individuals to exercise more control over the investment of the mandatory saving that is the bedrock of their retirement income.

Even though individuals should control their own lives as much as possible, some limits are necessary. The gains from individual control must be weighed against other goals, such as keeping administrative costs reasonable and ensuring pension adequacy. Administrative costs and the variability of returns rise when people invest in diverse assets. Because record keeping and mailings cost the same for large and small accounts, overhead costs are proportionately larger when the average account is small than when it is large. Costs are minimized if account administration is centralized in a single entity. They are somewhat higher if participants can choose among a few financial institutions and much higher if many fund managers are competing for accounts and workers can shift their accounts from manager to manager. Similarly, administrative costs are low if workers are limited to a few indexed funds and increase steadily as investment choice is broadened. The annual costs of a completely decentralized system like that of current IRAs might exceed those of a centralized system like Social Security by as much as 1 to 2 percent of funds held on deposit, a difference that lowers lifetime accumulations 20 to 40 percent.

Allowing individuals wide latitude over the investment of their mandatory retirement savings has risks as well as benefits. Even the sophisticated sometimes fall prey to scams or exercise bad judgment. But most Americans have little experience managing investment funds. Less than half of the U.S. population has a tax-sheltered, individually managed retirement account. Only one-fifth directly own mutual fund shares or common stocks. Fewer than one in five has accumulated liquid assets equal to the income they earn in one year.[4]

These facts do not mean that private accounts are a bad idea— the long-run growth of U.S. financial markets testifies to their potential. Rather, administrative costs and the limited investment experience of the average worker suggest that relying exclusively on loosely regulated personal retirement accounts is risky. Some investors would take excessive risks in the search for high returns. Others would be excessively cautious, choosing low-yielding assets that would produce inadequate retirement benefits. Unless sales practices of financial institutions authorized to manage personal retirement accounts were tightly regulated, some investors would succumb to sharp sales practices, and marketing costs would eat up a substantial portion of the returns. Experience in the United Kingdom supports such concerns.[5] Even with extensive protections, individuals would be exposed to the risks of fluctuations in interest rates and asset prices that can undermine the adequacy of what once looked like a sufficient nest egg.

LABOR MARKET EFFICIENCY

Advocates of personal accounts claim that a privatized system would distort workers' decisions about how much to work less than Social Security does. They argue that workers are well aware of the payroll taxes they must pay, but have little understanding of, and therefore place little value on, the benefits they will ultimately receive in return for these payments. Thus, the system as a whole is perceived primarily as a tax that, like other taxes on earnings, distorts labor supply by reducing the returns workers receive for additional work effort. Distortions under a privatized system, they feel, would be smaller because workers would better understand, and feel more secure about, the benefits that contributions to their retirement accounts finance.

This argument is somewhat oversimplified. The same myopia that makes mandatory saving desirable will cause workers to undervalue future benefits from individual accounts just as they do Social Security benefits. Nevertheless, it is possible that labor supply could be affected differently if workers have a greater appreciation of the benefits they hope to receive from their personal accounts versus those they will receive from Social Security. To the extent that misunderstanding is the problem, education is the answer.

The principal difference in work incentives between a privatized system and Social Security arises from variations in the social assistance each system might provide. On average, the benefits per dollar of taxes paid would be the same under the two systems, if reserves are similarly invested (apart from administrative costs). But income redistribution necessarily entails taxing some people to provide assistance to others. The labor supply distortions that arise from taxes and transfers are an inescapable price of social assistance. The more social assistance—for low earners, large families, nonworking spouses, and widows and widowers—the more the distortions. If the effects on labor supply of Social Security vary from those of a privatized system, the differences arise either from lack of information or from differences in real social assistance.

INCREASED NATIONAL SAVING

The primary benefit claimed for privatization is that it would boost national saving. As we emphasized in Chapter 4, the case for raising national saving is strong. Increased saving, and the higher rate of capital formation that this saving would generate, would boost the growth of output per worker and help the nation shoulder the costs of a gradually increasing dependent population. Replacing a pay-as-you-go Social Security system with fully funded private accounts would probably boost national saving. But so too would a buildup of Social Security reserves.

Which approach would raise saving more? The answer, alas, is a resounding: Nobody knows! To explain why this is the case, we must examine the three conditions that determine how much new saving would result from a dollar added to the Social Security trust funds' reserves and a dollar deposited in a personal retirement account—the yield on the two balances, budget offsets, and private offsets.

Yields. If the choice is between contributions to personal retirement accounts and equal additions to Social Security reserves, the one that has the higher yield will grow fastest and tend to add more to saving since all the contributions and investment returns accumulated in the two are held until paid out as pensions.[6] Current law requires Social Security to invest its reserves only in securities guaranteed as to principal and interest by the government.[7] These securities tend to yield less than the assets held by private pension funds—corporate bonds, stocks, and real estate. In other words, yield differences arise from restrictions imposed on the trust funds' managers, and have nothing to do with privatization. If Social Security could invest its additional reserves in the same assets private fund managers normally select, it would earn similar returns and generate as much saving.

Budget Offsets. The buildup of Social Security reserves may tempt elected officials to raise government spending or cut taxes, thereby reducing the effect of accumulation of the trust funds on national saving (see Box 5–1). To the extent that buildup in the trust funds does not trigger tax cuts or spending increases, additions to Social Security reserves boost national saving by raising unified budget surpluses or reducing deficits. Keeping the operations of

---

BOX 5–1
THE ABCs OF NATIONAL SAVING

National saving is the difference between what the nation produces and what it consumes, publicly and privately. It consists of real resources that are available for investment in new office buildings and stores, industrial plants, warehouses, equipment, inventories, and residential structures. It is this real capital that adds to national productivity. Certificates of ownership—common stocks, bonds, mortgages, mutual fund shares, royalty contracts—are the counterparts of this real capital, but do not themselves add a scintilla to economic capacity. It is *real* capital that counts, not the value of *paper* capital.

To understand how an increase in funding of pensions can raise national saving, it helps to divide total national saving (NS) into four components: private saving for retirement (P_{RS}), private saving for other purposes (P_O), government saving under Social Security (G_{SS}), and government saving in the rest of its operations (G_O).

$$NS = P_{RS} + P_O + G_{SS} + G_O$$

Social Security surpluses increase trust fund reserves and raise G_{SS}. This will not raise national saving, however, if elected officials use Social Security reserves to underwrite equal increases in deficits (or reductions in surpluses) on other operations of government, which would show up as a decline in G_O. Mandatory private retirement saving will boost P_{RS}, but this will not raise national saving if people cut back on other forms of saving, P_O, equally. The effect on national saving of adding the same amount to P_{RS} or to G_{SS} will be identical as long as the offsets to P_O and G_O are the same.

The central question in the debate about whether accumulating reserves in Social Security (that is, adding to G_{SS}) or in personal retirement accounts (that is, adding to P_{RS}) will add more to national saving boils down to whether the offsets in P_O or in G_O will be larger.

Social Security separate in financial presentations and in policy debate involving other tax and expenditure decisions would make it more likely that any reserve accumulation will boost saving. We describe ways to effect such a separation in Chapter 6.

Private Offsets. The creation of personal retirement accounts could either raise or lower other household saving. Personal retirement accounts might advertise the virtues of saving and thereby increase it. Business-sponsored programs to explain their 401(k) pension plans have raised saving.[8] They heighten people's awareness of the advantages of saving, showing that repeated deposits, even small ones, can grow to significant balances over time, and create a workplace climate in which saving is respected and valued. Periodic statements of personal account balances could also demonstrate the power of compound investment returns. Such reports, together with reminders about the dangers of saving too little, can teach frugality and lead workers to save more outside their personal retirement accounts. Of course, one does not need to privatize Social Security to undertake private and public campaigns to educate workers on the virtues of saving.

While this "consciousness-raising" argument carries some force, the bulk of economic research suggests that growing balances in private accounts would tend to raise consumption—that is, lower saving—because asset owners feel wealthier. Most people now express great skepticism that they will receive all the Social Security benefits current law promises. If they receive a periodic statement showing that their very own personal retirement account balances are large and rising, they are likely to feel more secure about their retirement incomes, raise consumption, and reduce other saving.

Thus, creating private retirement accounts would *probably* reduce other saving. How much is unclear. Experience with tax provisions designed to encourage retirement saving is worrisome. After Congress created tax incentives, like IRAs, to promote individual retirement saving, saving in tax-sheltered individual accounts rose from nothing to 1.4 percent of national product during the 1986–93 period. Unfortunately, voluntary saving, apart from retirement saving and life insurance, vanished entirely, dropping from 3 percent of national product in the 1970s to net *borrowing* of 0.2 percent of national product.[9] While many factors other than the advent of tax-sheltered saving influenced private saving during this period, one cannot escape the troubling possibility that many people may have just shifted assets and saving from taxable accounts to the new tax-sheltered vehicles. This episode serves as a warning: If people are forced to save in one form they may cut back in another.

It is impossible to forecast reliably the net effect of these various incentives and offsets. Replacement of the government's largest program, one that provides most retirees with most of their income, is bound to have unforeseen consequences. But one effect is likely— accumulating pension reserves should raise national saving somewhat, whether reserves are held in Social Security trust funds or personal retirement accounts. Which form of reserve accumulation will raise saving most is impossible to predict because the results depend sensitively on plan details and on behaviors—of private individuals and elected officials—that no one can estimate with any degree of certainty.

POLITICAL CONFLICT

The specter of intergenerational conflict has been much in the news in recent years. Some people fear an ugly political scrum between greedy geezers struggling to hold on to their benefits and beleaguered workers fighting to protect themselves and their families from onerous taxes. It is hard to know how seriously to take such apprehensions. Opinion polls report that young and middle-aged adults strongly support Social Security and Medicare, even as they voice concern over whether these programs will actually deliver benefits promised to them. The young are almost as likely as the elderly to feel that these programs should be enriched rather than cut back.[10] This situation is unlikely to change, as elderly and disabled beneficiaries are always the parents and grandparents of active workers who care not only about their taxes but also about the continued financial security of their elderly relatives.

Privatization could eventually end the potential for intergenerational conflict over Social Security taxes and benefits because each generation would pay fully for its own retirement. This advantage, however, would be slow in coming. For several decades, in fact, privatization could intensify intergenerational conflict, as young workers would have to support previous generations of workers who would be receiving diminished Social Security benefits at the same time as they were contributing to their own retirement accounts. This extra burden might well provoke resentment among younger workers. Some would consider it "unfair" to force them to pay the retirement costs of two generations, especially when some of the benefits for retirees would be going to people with significant private pensions and asset income.

Updating Contribution Rates. Privatization would raise new and potentially divisive issues for public discussion. Instead of debating whether to impose added taxes on workers or to cut benefits, people would argue over how much each person should be required to contribute to his or her own account. If contribution rates were held constant, changes in wage growth, in asset values, and in interest rates could produce large changes in replacement rates, as we illustrated in Chapter 3. To prevent such large fluctuations, sizable adjustments would have to be made periodically in the required individual contribution rate. And when asset prices fell, Congress would come under pressure to compensate those who were about to retire (see Box 5–2 for a past example of such pressures).

The problem can be illustrated by examining the changes in contribution rates that would have been required under a hypothetical defined-contribution retirement plan that started operations in 1953 and was designed to provide pensions that replaced half of preretirement earnings. If the contribution rate was adjusted once each decade to keep the plan headed for that 50 percent replacement rate, contributions would have varied from a low of 5.2 percent to a high of 39 percent of earnings.[11] With less frequent adjustments, pensions would have fallen well short of or greatly exceeded the target replacement rate. This analysis does not reflect the sharp variations in asset values that occur within and between years, described in Chapter 3, which would have caused replacement rates for workers reaching retirement age just a few months or years apart to differ greatly if personal retirement account assets were invested exclusively in common stocks. Of course, most people would choose to invest their personal account balances in a portfolio containing different kinds of assets. But the historical record shows that the value of a balanced portfolio also varies a good deal from year to year. Therefore, pensions for workers with similar contribution records and investment patterns would vary depending on asset levels when they retire or become disabled.

Government guarantees of minimum returns on their investments or minimum benefits could protect defined-contribution pensioners from drops in asset values or imprudent investments. Such a safety net would probably be subject to a means test to limit costs, to concentrate assistance on the truly needy, and to minimize the incentive for workers to pursue excessively risky investment strategies, safe in the knowledge that they could keep high returns while the government, in effect, insured them against loss. Means tests increase complexity and administrative costs. In addition, a guarantee would have to be financed by raising taxes or cutting other government spending, measures that would raise intergenerational tensions similar to those allegedly facing Social Security.

BOX 5–2
THE PECULIAR POLITICS OF "NOTCH BABIES"

Before 1975, Social Security benefits were not automatically adjusted for inflation. Instead, Congress periodically passed legislation to offset the effects of inflation. Doing so took time and bother, but it had its reward—voters were grateful. Not surprisingly, bills to raise Social Security benefits were enacted mostly just before congressional elections. Democrats controlled Congress and got most of the credit. Republicans steamed. Partly to eliminate this opportunity for political advantage, Republicans urged that benefits be automatically adjusted for inflation. The proposal was clearly a good idea on substantive grounds. By the 1970s, inflation was becoming more of a problem than it had been since World War II. Why make the retired and disabled wait until Congress got around to acting? With bipartisan support, legislation was passed in 1972 that raised benefits by a whopping 20 percent and called for automatic "indexation" of Social Security starting in 1975.

Unfortunately, the adjustment formula Congress adopted was flawed. Congress was not at fault. The formula was the same one the actuaries had used in the past to design ad hoc legislated increases. It worked well enough when inflation was low, but provided excessive adjustments when inflation was high. When inflation was more than 1 to 2 percent, as it was with disturbing consistency during the 1970s, replacement rates—the ratio of benefits to average wages—rose relentlessly. For the average earner, replacement rates rose from 34 percent in 1970 to a peak of 54 percent for those who turned 62 in 1978. But payroll tax receipts rose no faster than average wages, and deficits began to develop.

Something had to be done. The Carter administration proposed a formula that adjusted benefits correctly for inflation and called on Congress to reduce replacement rates for people who reached retirement age *after* 1977 to what they would have been if the inflation adjustment had been made correctly all along. But it did not propose, and Congress did not enact, any change in benefits for those who had reached retirement age *between* 1972 and 1977 and had benefited from the flawed indexation mechanism.

This decision spared Congress one problem—the need to take benefits away from people who already had reached retirement age. But it created another—a "notch." Benefits were approximately 10 percent smaller on the average for people who reached retirement age just after 1977 than for those who reached retirement just before. Those affected adversely came to be known as the "notch babies." The exact differential between their benefits and those of people who became eligible just before 1977 depended on individual circumstances. But, whatever the differential, those on the short end felt shortchanged. They formed protest clubs. They filled congressional mailbags with letters venting outrage. Commissions were established to analyze the problem. Congressional committees held hearings. Members introduced "corrective" legislation. Not surprisingly, only two of the 113 "corrective" bills would have lowered the erroneous excess benefits paid to those born before 1917. The others would have raised the correctly calculated benefits of those born after 1916.

Continued on the next page

> BOX 5–2 (CONTINUED)
> THE PECULIAR POLITICS OF "NOTCH BABIES"
>
> In the end, Congress resisted the protests of the notch babies. Privately, many members understood that the case for raising benefits for the notch babies was insubstantial. Outside organizations, including a blue-ribbon panel created by the National Academy of Social Insurance, made clear that the claims of the notch babies were unjustified. And budget pressures made any expenditure increases hard to justify. In the end, Congress left the 1977 legislation alone. But the furor created over the 10 percent benefit differential that arose from the flawed adjustment formula serves as a warning of the problems that might arise if price fluctuations in financial markets cause even larger benefit differentials under a privatized system.

Social Adequacy. Income redistribution is likely to become a more divisive issue under a privatized system than it is today. The Social Security benefit formula simultaneously provides pensions for all beneficiaries and additional social assistance for low earners. Some privatization plans maintain benefits for low earners through a separate component in a dual system. For example, under one plan, retired workers who had been employed a minimum number of years would receive a flat benefit financed by payroll taxes, in addition to a pension derived from personal retirement accounts that were financed by mandatory individual deposits. The combination could approximate the distribution of benefits under the current system. However, all the redistribution would be concentrated in the flat benefit component, and as the ratio of retirees to active workers increases, the payroll tax rate required to support the flat benefit would increase, raising pressures similar to those that some feel will lead to generational warfare if the current Social Security system is maintained. Creating a dual system does nothing to reduce this source of potential intergenerational conflict. It would simply focus this tension on the component of the new system that disproportionately serves low earners.

To sum up, replacing Social Security with a system of individual accounts would change, but not necessarily cool, debate about retirement policy. Pensions are so costly to society and so important to the elderly, disabled, and survivors that political debate on retirement policy will always be a hot political issue. Privatization would eventually end debates over how to close the projected deficits in the partially funded Social Security system because the benefit obligations of defined-contribution plans are limited to accumulated reserves in personal retirement accounts. Nevertheless, other contentious issues would remain to inflame political passions. One would be whether to compensate retirees who end up with inadequate pensions because of bad investment decisions or downturns in financial markets. Others include how to manage the transition and how to sustain the retirement incomes of low-wage workers whose personal security accounts provide insufficient benefits.

RISKS OF PRIVATIZATION

A switch from Social Security to privatized personal retirement accounts carries a number of risks. We have already described several. Variability of investment returns could leave some workers with inadequate pensions and would assuredly produce large variations in pensions among people who had made similar contributions. Unanticipated inflation could erode the value of pensions of older retirees. Political support for the crucial antipoverty role that Social Security has played for over a half-century could atrophy. Two other problems associated with privatization deserve more attention—administrative costs and individual ignorance about financial markets.

ADMINISTRATIVE COSTS

All pension plans, public or private, must collect and keep track of individual workers' contributions, distribute information to participants, manage assets, determine eligibility for benefits, and pay retirement benefits. Expenditures to perform these tasks unavoidably reduce the growth of account balances and should therefore be kept as low as possible, consistent with adequate service.

The Social Security Administration (SSA) sets a high standard for administrative efficiency and customer service. The total cost of administering Social Security retirement and survivor's insurance averages only about 0.7 percent of benefit payments.[12] SSA enjoys economies of scale that private plans cannot match. Practically all of SSA's costs go for clerical functions—keeping track of individuals' earnings, distributing reports to participants, and paying benefits.[13]A small amount represents the costs the Treasury Department incurs collecting payroll taxes. Private employers also incur few extra costs collecting and remitting the Social Security payroll taxes because they must keep track of workers' earnings anyway to compute business and personal income, Medicare, and unemployment compensation taxes.

Running a system of personal retirement accounts would be more expensive than running Social Security. How much more expensive depends on the type of plan. The principal extra administrative costs of privatized alternatives arise from selling expenses, fees for managing assets, and costs for verifying the accuracy of records. Social Security incurs no selling costs because the plan is universal and mandatory. The cost of managing the trust funds' reserves is also trivial because the balances in the Social Security trust funds are invested centrally only in securities guaranteed as to principal and interest by the U.S. government. And verification costs are limited because earnings credits are linked to wages reported for income tax purposes. In addition, because Social Security benefits depend only on average earnings, which are calculated once at age 60, errors are relatively easy to correct. In contrast, personal account balances would have to be verified repeatedly because miscredited amounts would compound over time.

The 1997 Advisory Council on Social Security estimated that costs for individually managed plans that would permit people to invest freely in stocks, bonds, or mutual funds, as well as in investment products offered by insurance companies or brokerage houses, would average 1 percent of funds managed per year—*this would be equal to a front-end loading charge of 20 percent*. This IRA-type of privatized system would also cost employers substantially more than Social Security does if they were required to remit funds directly to a number of different financial intermediaries rather than send payroll tax contributions to the Treasury, along with other taxes that would have to be paid anyway. Small businesses and firms employing low-wage workers would be especially burdened. The 5.4 million employers that do not use computerized payroll systems would find it costly to make timely deposits into their workers' various investment accounts. Moreover, many of these deposits would be small. If 2 percent of earnings were designated for personal retirement accounts and each worker maintained only one account, half of the deposits employers would make each month would be less than $31 and one-fifth would be less than $9. Relative to the amounts involved, employer and financial institution administrative costs would be high. Finally, if workers in such a plan could choose whether to convert fund balances into annuities, they would face an additional charge that is estimated to average between 10 and 20 percent of the price of the annuity.[14]

Not all privatization plans would involve such high administrative costs. The Advisory Council estimated that government-managed plans modeled after the federal employees' Thrift Savings Plan (TSP) would have annual costs close to those of the TSP—that is, about, 0.105 percent of funds managed. Several factors suggest that this estimate may be too low. The TSP deals with only federal agencies, all of which are computerized, not with millions of small and large employers. These agencies, not TSP, provide many account services and education. Furthermore, job turnover in the federal government is low, and wages, and thus contribution amounts, are relatively high. In addition, federal personnel records contain family information that a pension plan would need if a worker got divorced.[15] Taking account of all these factors, one analyst has estimated that total administrative costs for a TSP-type plan would be equivalent to a front-end loading charge of 6 to 9 percent.

Nonetheless, costs for this type of plan would be substantially lower than those for the IRA-type plan for several reasons. The TSP-type plan limits investment choice to a small number of passively managed, no-load index funds—such as a stock market index fund, a corporate bond index fund, and a government bond fund. A few financial institutions would be selected through competitive bids to manage the stock and corporate bond funds. The government would prohibit the management firms from attempting to influence investors' choices through aggressive selling or advertising, and account balances would have to be paid as indexed annuities upon retirement. Such a centralized system of individual accounts would capture many of the economies of scale in administration enjoyed by Social Security today.

A system of individually managed accounts could bring huge revenues to the financial services industry. The initial annual flow of investment funds into a privatized system that channeled 2 percent of earnings into private accounts would be about $75 billion. If administrative costs average 1 percent of accumulated funds, the annual revenue from managing these funds would reach $14 billion after ten years and rise steadily thereafter. Nonetheless, it is unclear whether this business would be profitable. Small accounts are costly to administer. Any whiff of scandal would bring congressional hearings and federal regulation that may well affect the other operations of the financial industry.

Any comparison of administrative costs should encompass the whole system. Social Security's administrative structure handles three categories of benefits—retirement pensions, survivor's benefits, and disability payments. This arrangement provides economies of scope—one agency for three programs—and of scale—176 million insured workers and 44 million beneficiaries. Privatization plans would unavoidably require duplicate administrative structures and costs because most privatization plans would retain Social Security retirement benefits for at least several decades and continue survivor's and disability insurance permanently.

PERSONAL CONTROL OVER ACCOUNTS

Advocates of privatization lay particular stress on the value of individual control of personal retirement accounts, both before and after retirement. With individual control, however, come important economic and political problems. If individuals own identified personal accounts and are free to determine how these funds are invested, they are likely to regard these accounts as personal property similar to other personal saving. Pressure will build to allow withdrawals before retirement. The experience with IRAs is instructive. Originally, nearly all IRA withdrawals made before age 59 1/2 were subject both to regular income tax and to a 10 percent penalty tax. In 1996, the law was changed to permit penalty-free withdrawals to meet large medical expenses and to buy health insurance if the account holder was unemployed. The Taxpayers Relief Act of 1997 liberalized the law further by permitting penalty-free withdrawals to cover expenses associated with the purchase of a first home and for postsecondary educational expenses of a family member. Under a privatized system, similar arguments will be made—that account holders should be allowed to withdraw funds from their retirement accounts to pay for personal health care expenses if they or a family member is seriously ill, to pay educational expenses, and for other purposes. As restrictions are relaxed, it becomes more likely that personal account balances will be drawn down before retirement, defeating the very purpose of the accounts and exposing the government to larger future welfare payments for those who have depleted their accounts.

The discretion that people are given over the use of their personal accounts at retirement also is problematic in a program to assure a basic retirement income. While some privatization schemes would require workers to convert account balances into annuities at retirement, others would permit people to withdraw funds in a lump sum when they retire or in a series of payments spread over several years. Still other plans would allow those who can support themselves in retirement through other income sources to leave their fund balances on deposit and bequeath them to their heirs at death. Because of adverse selection, giving people an option *not* to annuitize boosts costs for those who want annuities. To combat this risk, insurers must offer smaller annuities to everyone than would be possible if annuitization were mandatory.[16]

If annuitization were optional, some people would exhaust their savings and become public charges. In addition, people whose annuities would approximate the aggregate benefits from Supplemental Security Income benefits, food stamps, and other means-tested programs would face a perverse incentive not to annuitize. Instead, they could withdraw their savings over a few years, during which they could enjoy an elevated standard of living. After their savings were exhausted, they could fall back on welfare, where they would enjoy about the same income an annuity would have provided.

If people could hold their personal accounts until they die, so-called *retirement* accounts would become little more than devices people could use to escape taxes on investment income and to build their estates for their heirs. This feature would help only the wealthy.

PRIVATIZATION—A SUMMING UP

Converting Social Security retirement benefits to personal retirement accounts means replacing a defined-benefit pension system with a defined-contribution pension system. This shift would place on individual retirees a variety of financial market risks that Social Security now diffuses broadly across workers and taxpayers, both current and future. We believe that individuals are poorly equipped to handle these risks and that a defined-benefit pension should continue to serve as the source of the nation's basic retirement pensions.

On the other hand, reserve accumulation in private accounts or in expanded Social Security trust funds could increase U.S. saving rates. Forcing the baby-boom generation, now in its prime working years, to shoulder a part of the burden of building these reserves would enrich the nation's capital stock, raise worker productivity, and offset some of the costs future workers will bear to support the baby boomers.

A system of supplementary personal retirement saving could also be used to build up reserves. If such a course were followed, the new program should be additional to a basic defined-benefit pension, such as Social Security. For reasons we shall explain in the next chapter, we can see no compelling case for scaling back Social Security benefits to "make room" for a supplementary system. Such "carve-out" plans would cut assured benefits that are by no means generous to make room for supplementary benefits that force more risk on workers and pensioners and raise administrative costs. Whatever the size of a new program of mandatory personal saving, rules should restrict investments to no-load index funds managed in a manner similar to the Thrift Savings Plan of federal employees. The average returns on funds as large as those any mandatory saving program would generate cannot deviate much from the market-wide average rate of return. Since nothing can significantly boost this return, anything spent on administration, beyond the bare minimum necessary for speedy investment, is pure waste and should be avoided. Enriching pensioners, not financial institutions, should be the objective of pension reform.

6

THE CASE FOR PRESERVING SOCIAL SECURITY: HOW SHOULD IT BE DONE?

From small beginnings, Social Security has become the largest and most popular program of the federal government. Its benefits account for 5.3 percent of the nation's personal income and over half of the income for two-thirds of the elderly. Because of Social Security, millions of older workers can now afford to retire while still active and healthy. The program's financial support allows most retired and disabled people to live modestly but independently. It thereby spares beneficiaries the indignity of becoming financially dependent on government welfare, private charity, or children, and spares millions of nonelderly the burden of supporting dependent relatives. Because benefits are provided as inflation-protected annuities, recipients need not worry that market fluctuations, inflation, or an especially long life will rob them of their financial independence. Without much controversy, Social Security has become the government's most powerful antipoverty policy. Without its benefits, half of the elderly would be poor; with these benefits, only 10.8 percent are.[1]

Although Social Security is important and successful, even its most ardent supporters acknowledge that the program has shortcomings. Social Security's structure reflects the economic, social, and demographic conditions of mid-twentieth-century America, not the circumstances of a nation entering the twenty-first century. A modernized and strengthened Social Security system, not the existing one, should be the program compared to the fully or partially privatized approaches that have been proposed as replacements for the current Social Security system.

Of the many changes, small and large, that could strengthen and modernize the program, the most important are:

◆   to modify benefits provided to spouses in recognition of the increased labor force participation of women;

◆   to improve the adequacy of benefits for older survivors;

◆   to make the annual cost-of-living adjustments more accurate;

◆   to increase the age of initial eligibility for retirement benefits, in recognition of the improved health and longevity of the elderly; and

◆   to speed the accumulation of financial reserves and diversify the assets in which Social Security reserves are invested.

Taken together, the changes would restore and sustain approximate long-run balance between the system's revenues and expenditures.

STRENGTHS OF THE CURRENT SYSTEM

Before describing ways to strengthen the existing system, we review four attributes of Social Security that privatization could jeopardize but that we feel are particularly important to preserve.

SOCIAL ASSISTANCE

Preservation of the extra financial assistance Social Security provides to low earners and other vulnerable participants is essential. Such assistance ensures that low earners receive benefits sufficient to sustain financial independence in retirement. Compared either to benefits abroad or to domestic measures of income adequacy, pensions provided by the

---

BOX 6–1
THE BENEFIT FORMULA

Social Security replaces more of the pay of low earners than of high earners because it provides a larger payback on their first few thousand dollars of average earnings than on higher amounts. For example, benefits for workers who will claim benefits at age 65 in the year 2001 will equal 90 percent of annual earnings up to $5,724, 32 percent of annual earnings from $5,724 to $34,500, and 15 percent of annual earnings from $35,500 to $68,400, the maximum earnings subject to payroll taxes in 1998 when these workers turned age 62.

Each year the maximum earnings subject to tax and the income ranges used in the benefit formula are raised by the growth in average earnings in jobs covered by Social Security. Between 1997 and 1998, for example, the top of the 90 percent range rose from $5,460 to $5,724, a 4.8 percent increase. The following annual pension amounts and replacement rates illustrate how the benefit formula worked in 1998 for those retiring at age 65 after working at least 35 years at various earnings levels.

Average Adjusted Earnings	Pension (Dollars)	Replacement Rate (Percent)
Low Earnings—45 percent of the average wage ($12,164)	$ 6,824	56
Average wage ($27,026)	11,270	42
High Earnings—160 percent of the average wage ($43,268)	14,538	34
Maximum taxable earnings ($65,279)	16,124	25

---

current system are far from generous (see Box 6–1). For workers with average earnings, the U.S. replacement rate is less than half those of the French and Dutch systems and less than two-thirds of those offered by the Belgian, Italian, German, and Spanish systems. Overall, the replacement rate for early retirees in the United States ranked tenth among eleven nations examined in one study, even though the United States had the highest age of initial eligibility.[2] Compared to official U.S. poverty thresholds, benefits are parsimonious. A worker retiring in 1996 after a lifetime of year-round work at the minimum wage received a pension that was slightly under the poverty threshold for a single person; a minimum-wage married retiree received a benefit that was just above the poverty threshold for a couple.[3] Benefits of average earners are less than 1.5 times the poverty threshold if they start drawing benefits at age 65, and are only 16 percent over the poverty threshold if they start benefits at age 62. If pensions were proportional to earnings or payroll tax payments, benefits for low earners would fall by over 25 percent. Poverty among the elderly, disabled, and survivors would increase. Welfare expenditures would rise. And many young and middle-aged workers would have to support parents, siblings, and other relatives who now manage independently.

The current benefit rules of the Social Security system favor not only low earners but also survivors, spouses, and divorcees who have had no or limited earnings. Later in this chapter, we describe desirable modifications in benefits available to these groups.

A completely privatized system cannot offer these forms of assistance. It would have to be supplemented with a separate government program that provided extra benefits to vulnerable groups. By placing social assistance in a distinct program, however, the integration of pensions and social assistance, which lies at the heart of Social Security, would be broken, and the social assistance program could come to be regarded as welfare, a category of government spending that has had little sustained political support in the United States.

INFLATION PROTECTION

Inflation protection is a second important aspect of Social Security that should be preserved. Each December, Social Security benefits are raised enough to compensate for price increases that have taken place during the previous year.[4] In the past, no major private pension plan offered comparable protection because long-run inflation is unpredictable and the financial risks of guaranteeing inflation-protected "real" annuities could bankrupt even the strongest private insurance companies. In 1997, the Treasury began to issue "indexed" securities—bonds that pay a fixed interest yield, plus compensation for the inflation that has occurred over the previous year. This innovation has made it possible for private insurance companies to offer real annuities backed up by government index bonds, but none has yet done so. As a result, Social Security remains the only source of retirement income that is insulated from the risk of unanticipated inflation and guaranteed to continue as long as the pensioners live.

Wage Risk

Because Social Security benefits vary less than proportionately with earnings, they provide a kind of pension insurance. Furthermore, benefits depend on a worker's average lifetime earnings, not on when the worker receives the earnings. Workers who have the same earnings averaged over their lifetimes receive the same Social Security benefits irrespective of their year-to-year pattern of earnings, which will be affected by how long they stay in school, mid-career breaks to raise children, and spells of unemployment.

Defined-contribution pensions depend critically on workers' earning patterns, which determine when contributions are made to personal retirement accounts. This is because the compounding of investment returns means that a dollar contributed when a worker is young will have a much greater impact than a dollar contributed just before retirement. Therefore, workers with similar average lifetime earnings who have made similar contributions to their retirement accounts can end up with vastly different pensions.

Financial Market Protection

Under Social Security, changes in asset values and interest rates do not directly affect benefits of *individual* workers, which depend on each worker's earnings and the benefit formula. The rate of return earned on the trust funds affects overall benefits because, over the long run, pension costs cannot exceed revenues. While changes in investment yields are important, the effects of fluctuations in asset prices on financial balance are surprisingly small because long-term financial balance depends principally on projected payroll tax revenues and benefit expenditures, as noted in Chapter 3.

Since the function of social insurance is to assure a basic income, we believe it is vital to continue to link pensions to stable quantities, such as a worker's lifetime earnings, not to highly volatile prices in financial markets. While it is important to invest Social Security reserves so that they yield high returns—and we indicate below ways to manage such investments—it is also important to make sure that risks of market fluctuations are broadly shared and not borne by individual pensioners.

STRENGTHENING SOCIAL
SECURITY FOR THE FUTURE

Social Security faces a projected long-term deficit that must be closed. As we noted in Chapter 4, the size of this fiscal shortfall is modest compared to past changes in the cost of Social Security. While it is technically possible to close the gap entirely through payroll tax increases, we reject this approach not only because reluctance to raise taxes is widespread and strong, but also because some modifications in Social Security are desirable to take account of the social and economic changes that have occurred since the basic structure of the system was laid down over half a century ago. The following recommendations would close the projected long-term deficit and make Social Security better reflect current social and economic conditions, while preserving Social Security's fundamental character. Table 6–1 lists the contribution that each of the proposed changes would make to closing the long-term deficit that remains after recent improvements in the way inflation is measured are incorporated in the Trustees' projections.

SPOUSE'S BENEFITS

From its inception Social Security has provided all workers, men and women alike, benefits based on their own earnings. In 1939, one year before the first worker's benefits were paid, Congress added a spouse's benefit equal to half of the primary worker's benefit for wives or husbands who had no or limited lifetime earnings. This treatment of spouses, which provides larger benefits for retired couples than for single retirees, dates from an era when most married women stayed home to care for children. Over the next few decades, most married women received the spouse's benefit because few had sufficient earnings to qualify them for a larger worker's benefit.

As the proportion of women working outside the home increased, the spouse's benefit came to cause what analysts call the "lesser-earner problem." Like other workers, lesser earners—usually wives—owe payroll taxes from their first dollar of earnings and become entitled to benefits after forty quarters of covered work. However, retirement benefits are only increased when the benefit based on their own earnings exceeds half of the primary worker's benefit.[5] Even then, the

Table 6–1
Closing the Projected Long-term Social Security Deficit

	Deficit or Change in Deficit as Percent of Payroll	Proportion of Adjusted Long-term Deficit Closed
Projected long-term deficit—1998 Trustees Report	2.19	n.a.
Effects of correcting the Consumer Price Index	-.45	n.a.
Adjusted long-term deficit	1.74	n.a.
Program Changes		
1. Gradually reduce spouse's benefits from one-half to one-third of the worker's benefits and raise benefits for surviving spouses to three-quarters of the couple's combined benefit.	+.15	-9
2. Cut benefits by increasing the unreduced benefit age—raise the age to 67 by 2011 rather than by 2022 and thereafter raise the age at which unreduced benefits are paid to keep the fraction of adult life spent in retirement constant.	-.49	28
3. Increase the initial age of eligibility from 62 to 64 by 2011 and thereafter raise the age of initial eligibility at the same pace as the unreduced benefit age.	-.23	13
4. Increase the period over which earnings are averaged from thirty-five to thirty-eight years.	-.25	14
5. Cover all newly hired state and local employees.	-.21	12
6. Tax Social Security benefits the same as private pension income.	-.36	21
7. Gradually invest the trust funds' balances that exceed 150 percent of yearly benefits in common stocks and corporate bonds.	-1.20	69
Total Program Changes	**-2.59**	**148**

Source: Estimates from the Office of the Actuary, Social Security Administration.

benefit increment above the spouse's benefit is small relative to the payroll taxes they have contributed to the system (see Box 6–2). This arrangement favors married women (or men) who do not work for pay. It does not discriminate against workers of either sex because they are always entitled to benefits based on their earnings records.

The simplest and least costly way to end the lesser-earner problem would be to eliminate the spouse's benefit altogether. However, this step would significantly reduce benefits for the many older couples in which one spouse worked outside the home little or not at all. It would also make it far more costly for one parent to stay home to care for the children. But a large majority of mothers, even those with preschool children, now work, and that proportion has been rising. A gradual reduction in the spouse's benefit over a decade or so from one-half of the principal earner's benefit to one-third or even one-quarter would free up funds that could be used to lower the projected long-term deficit or applied to improving other benefits along lines we outline below.[6]

Some observers favor a more far-reaching change called "earnings sharing." Earnings of a couple would be pooled, and each spouse would be credited with half of the total.[7] Since both spouses would have an earnings history, there would be no need for a separate spouse's benefit. Earnings sharing would protect divorced spouses who earned little outside the home and whose marriages did not last at least a decade, the period necessary under current law for divorcees to receive benefits based on their former spouse's earnings record.[8] This feature of earnings sharing is of some importance since about half of all marriages end in divorce and close to two-thirds of failed marriages last less than ten years.

Earnings sharing would lower benefits for many and could create difficulties for some. In one-earner couples, retirement might be difficult until both spouses were old enough to qualify for pensions, since the pension of the primary earner would be reduced by shifting some of his or her earnings to the lesser earner. Where the primary earner was much older than the spouse, this feature could create a major hardship. Furthermore, if earnings sharing were adopted, something would have to be done to make sure that half of the couple's earnings did not vanish with the first spouse's death. Possible solutions include providing survivors with three-quarters of the combined benefits of both spouses or permitting survivors to inherit the earnings credits of deceased spouses.

BOX 6–2
THE SPOUSE'S BENEFIT

Four couples, the Campbells, the Steins, the Smiths, and the Joneses, live in the same neighborhood. The husbands were all born in 1933 and have held similar jobs at the local factory where each earned, over his lifetime, the average worker's wage. In 1998, they turn age 65 and retire. Each husband receives a Social Security retirement benefit of $938 per month.

Sally Campbell has raised her children, taken care of her sick mother-in-law, and been an active volunteer at the church and Girl Scouts. But she never worked in the paid labor force. When her husband retires, she is entitled to a spouse's benefit of $469, one-half of her husband's benefit.

Judy Stein worked a bit before she had children and then dropped out of the paid workforce for several decades to raise her family and participate on the town council. She then worked part-time for a decade. Her earnings experience entitles her to a worker's benefit equal to 20 percent of her husband's benefit. Because this is less than the amount available under the spouse's benefit, she also receives a reduced spouse's benefit sufficient to bring her total benefit up to one-half of her husband's benefit. She and her husband have paid a bit more in Social Security taxes than the Campbells, but their overall benefits are the same.

Charlotte Smith raised her children while holding down a part-time job. She went back to work full-time when the youngest left for college. Her average lifetime earnings, however, amounted to only 29 percent of her husband's earnings. Although she earned well under half of what her husband earned, she is entitled to a retirement benefit equal to half of her husband's benefit. Although she and her husband have paid considerably more in payroll taxes into the system than have the Campbells, the benefits they receive are no larger.

Ruth Jones took a travel agency job just after leaving school and enjoyed it so much that she worked steadily full-time even while raising her children. Her average lifetime earnings and payroll tax payments equaled her husband's. As a result, she receives a retirement pension equal to her husband's. But while the Joneses have contributed twice as much to the Social Security system over the years as have the Campbells, their combined benefit is only one-third larger.

These examples illustrate the following facts:

1. Social Security treats couples at least as generously as it treats two single people with the same earnings.

2. The spouse's benefit is paid even if one spouse does not work at all.

3. Social Security does not discriminate against lesser earning spouses, most of whom are women. It discriminates in favor of the lesser earner (usually the woman) by paying her a benefit equal to half of the primary earner's (usually the man) benefit, even if her earnings were small or nonexistent.

We favor phasing down the spouse's benefit over a decade from one-half to one-third of the worker's benefit. Benefits for spouses who work intermittently or at low wages would be reduced less than for those who did not work outside the home.

SURVIVOR'S BENEFITS

Many elderly widows, widowers, and divorcees have very modest incomes. While 87 percent of aged couples had incomes at least one-and-a-half times the 1996 poverty threshold, only half of single elderly people living alone met this income threshold. The most important reasons for the income differential between single and married elderly lie outside the Social Security system. Some private pensions last only as long as the retired worker is alive. Even if the pension continues for survivors, its value falls because no private pension is fully adjusted for inflation.[9] In addition, investment income declines as the aged spend down their assets. Social Security survivor's benefits provide another explanation for the income differences. Under the current system, couples receive benefits 50 to 100 percent larger than those of surviving widows and widowers, while the poverty threshold for an elderly couple is only 26 percent higher than that for a single person.[10]

Liberalizing the survivor benefit would improve the economic lot of survivors, a goal of increasing importance as life expectancy lengthens. Providing survivors with three-quarters of the couple's combined benefit would increase support for most widows and widowers. When combined with the previous proposal to reduce the spouse's benefit from one-half to one-third of the primary worker's pension, this initiative would ensure survivors a higher benefit than does the current system if their earnings entitled them to a benefit equal to at least one-third of their spouses' pensions. Most women retiring in the future would gain from this change because most will have long earnings histories. The added costs associated with this proposal would be offset, in part, by the savings achieved by reducing the spouse's benefit (see Table 6–1).

THE AGE FOR UNREDUCED BENEFITS

In 1983, Congress enacted an across-the-board benefit cut that will grow to about 13 percent in 2022. The benefit cut took the form of a gradual increase from 65 to 67 in the age at which unreduced benefits are first paid. The first cuts were delayed until 2000. For people turning 62 in 2000 and the five succeeding years, the unreduced benefits age will increase by two months each year—an annual benefit cut of about 1 percent—until it reaches 66 for people turning age 62 in 2005. The same process will be repeated between 2017 and 2022, at which point the unreduced benefit age will be 67.[11] The 1983 legislation did not raise the age at which reduced benefits can be received.

Some policymakers and analysts would cut benefits still more by raising the age at which unreduced benefits are paid to 68, 70, or even later ages. The stated justification for additional increases is that life expectancy at age 65 has increased by more than four years since the program was enacted in 1935. Since these proposals do not call for any change in the age of initial eligibility, the linkage of life expectancy to the retirement age is misleading. They are simply benefit cuts.

Most people say that they oppose benefit cuts, which is not surprising considering that Social Security benefits are modest compared either to those of foreign nations or to our own poverty thresholds. Nonetheless, some benefit cuts will be necessary if revenue increases are not to bear the full burden of closing the projected long-term deficit. We propose that the benefit reduction enacted in 1983 be phased in without the twelve-year hiatus between 2005 and 2017. The cuts enacted in 1983 would be completed in 2011, not 2022. After 2011, we propose that benefits for workers who retire at any given age be cut gradually as life expectancy increases. Workers who spent the same proportion of their adult lives in retirement as those turning 62 in 2011 would receive unchanged benefits. In other words, if retirement represented one-fourth of adult life in 2011, a one-year increase in adult longevity would lead to the benefit cut associated with a nine-month increase in the age at which unreduced benefits are paid.[12] These changes would reduce the projected long-term deficit by 28 percent.

AGE OF INITIAL ELIGIBILITY FOR BENEFITS

When Social Security first began paying benefits, pensions were available only to those age 65 or older. Retirement benefits were made available at age 62 to women in 1956 and to men in 1961. Workers who claim benefits before age 65 receive permanently reduced pensions. A 62-year-old claimant, for example, receives an annuity 80 percent as large as he or she would have received by retiring at age 65.[13] The reduction factor was set so that an average worker would receive the same cumulative lifetime benefit no matter when, between the ages of 62 and 65, he or she decided to claim benefits. Since all workers differ in some ways from the "average" worker, many are unsure when it is best to claim benefits (see Box 6–3).

After the age of initial eligibility was lowered to 62, the proportion of people retiring before age 65 rose sharply. By 1997, some 70 percent of all retirement benefits were claimed before age 65. Because workers are retiring earlier and living longer, they are spending a larger part of their adult lives in retirement. This trend is unsurprising and should not be troubling—wealthier people buy more of the good things in life, and, surely, an old age with time for relaxation and grandchildren should rank high on most people's list of desirable objectives. Life expectancies of 65-year-old men and women are now higher—3.9 years and 5.9 years higher, respectively—than when Social Security benefits were first paid and are projected to increase an additional 1 year for women and 1.2 years for men over the next quarter of a century.

Because Congress did not raise the age of *initial eligibility* in 1983 when it increased the age at which *unreduced* benefits can be claimed, it set in motion changes that would lower the already meager benefits of early retirees, their spouses, and their survivors. A modest increase in the age at which Social Security benefits first become available could encourage somewhat later retirement and prevent people from agreeing to the large benefit reductions that come by claiming benefits early. We propose that the age of initial eligibility be increased from age 62 to age 64 over the same period that the age at which unreduced benefits are paid rises from 65 to 67. Such a change would assure more adequate retirement incomes for workers and their surviving spouses and would modestly lower program costs. It would also enlarge the labor force, boost national production, and reduce the burden of supporting the economically inactive.[14] This effect is significant because the annual growth rate of the working age population over the next three decades is projected to be less than one-third the pace of the past thirty years.

Like any other restriction on benefits, an increase in the age of initial eligibility produces some losers. Many workers yearn to retire,

---

BOX 6–3
SHOULD YOU CLAIM BENEFITS
AT AGE 62 OR WAIT UNTIL LATER?

Should you claim Social Security benefits at the first opportunity, just after you turn age 62? Or should you wait until age 65?

Delaying your claim increases the benefits you receive for the rest of your life. If you are the primary earner, it also increases the benefits to which your spouse will be entitled should you die first. The increase is 8 1/3 percent for each year you delay *claiming* benefits from age 62 to age 65 even if you do not work past age 62. That means that people who wait to age 65 receive a 25 percent larger benefit for the rest of their lives than they would receive if they claimed benefits at age 62. If you work past age 62 and those earnings are among the highest thirty-five of your career, your benefits will increase even more. These adjustments were set in place about three decades ago to compensate the *average beneficiary* of that time for delay. Since life expectancies have increased, the average worker now lives longer and is more likely to benefit from claiming benefits later than he or she would have been in the past.

What is true *on the average*, however, cannot be true for each person, since personal circumstances differ greatly. For two groups, claiming benefits early generally makes poor economic sense. The first group consists of people who are healthy and come from families that have longer-than-average life expectancies. For this group, it generally makes sense to wait to claim benefits until age 65 if health and economic circumstances permit. A 25 percent benefit increase that just compensates the average beneficiary with average life expectancy will provide a windfall for people who can expect to live longer than average.

The second group consists of principal earners who are married to spouses considerably younger than they are, especially if the earner is male. The lesser-earning spouse can anticipate an extended period of widowhood—a woman who is married to a man eight years older than she is can expect to spend about eleven years as a widow. Waiting increases the benefit the widow (or widower) will receive.

In both cases, waiting may turn out to be a mistake for particular individuals, and each person must consider his or her personal circumstances. Even the daily jogger who is the offspring of centenarians may be struck down unexpectedly. The young widow may die prematurely. But the odds favor waiting.

---

as indicated by the fact that nearly one-quarter of men still working at age 61 retire during the first year they become eligible for Social Security benefits. Some people find work particularly onerous or dull. For others Social Security is the financial margin that permits long-awaited retirement. For these groups, the delay in Social Security benefits would be a short-term loss, but would increase later retirement incomes. For still others—those with physical impairments or psychological problems—the delay in Social Security benefits can be a significant hardship. To protect this group, any increase in the age of initial eligibility for Social Security should be accompanied by easing the test for disability insurance benefits for those age 62 to 64, which would reduce the savings shown in Table 6–1.

AVERAGING PERIOD

Benefits are now based on the thirty-five years of highest adjusted earnings. Since most people work more than thirty-five years, counting more years would tighten the linkage between benefits and average career earnings. But lengthening the averaging period also lowers benefits because earnings for excluded years are necessarily lower than those of currently included years. The increase in the averaging period would cut benefits for the average worker by 3 percent and reduce the projected long-term deficit by 14 percent. The case for counting more years becomes stronger as the age at which unreduced benefits are first paid and the age of initial entitlement rise.[15]

INDEXING BENEFITS

Before 1972, Congress typically boosted benefits in election years to offset the erosion in the purchasing power of benefits that inflation had wrought since the last adjustment. In 1972, Congress adopted a formula to adjust benefits automatically. Many believe that the Consumer Price Index (CPI), which is used to adjust Social Security benefits, overstates inflation. The Bureau of Labor Statistics (BLS) has changed the way it calculates the CPI and has additional plans to improve the accuracy of the CPI. These changes have lowered the growth of the CPI, and this slowdown has reduced the projected long-term deficit of Social Security.[16]

The financial consequences of mismeasuring consumer prices are large because the CPI is used not only to adjust Social Security benefits, but also to update other government benefit programs, such as Supplemental Security Income, Veterans Compensation and Pensions, and Civil Service and Military Retirement and to adjust personal income tax exemptions, the standard deduction, and tax brackets. The Congressional Budget Office has estimated that if refinements in the measurement of consumer prices lowered growth of the CPI by 0.1 percentage points a year, spending after five years would be $2.4 billion lower and revenues would be $2.1 billion higher. Congress should provide the BLS with budget resources and personnel sufficient to make corrections expeditiously. Because the stakes are high and the issues are technical, it should also establish an advisory committee of nonpartisan outside experts to monitor progress.

While no one believes that inflation adjustments should be entirely abandoned, some analysts and elected officials have proposed that benefits should not be fully adjusted for inflation. Senator Daniel Patrick Moynihan (Democrat of New York) would adjust benefits 1 percentage point less than the measured CPI. Senator Bob Kerrey (Democrat of Nebraska) and former senator Alan Simpson (Republican of Wyoming) would provide full inflation adjustments only for the 30 percent of beneficiaries receiving the lowest benefits. Recipients of larger benefits would receive the same dollar increase paid to beneficiaries at the thirtieth percentile.

Beyond improving the accuracy of the CPI, we believe that curtailing inflation adjustments is unjustified. The Moynihan proposal would cause the purchasing power of all benefits to fall continuously the longer pensioners receive retirement, disability, or survivor payments. The Kerrey-Simpson proposal would deny full adjustments to people of modest means who receive relatively large Social Security benefits but have little other income. At the same time, it would give full inflation adjustments to beneficiaries who receive small Social Security checks but whose spouses have high incomes and to those who enjoy generous public pensions earned through long careers with one of the states or localities that remain outside of the Social Security system. Many long-term beneficiaries already face declining living standards as their other income sources become depleted. Social insurance should not make that problem worse, particularly considering the steady rise of real incomes among the economically active.

The long-run projections of the program's finances issued by the Social Security Administration's actuaries in 1998 omitted some announced modifications that would slow the CPI's increase. If these and certain other planned modifications had been incorporated in the long-run projections, the deficit would have been reduced from 2.19 percent to 1.74 percent of covered earnings (see Table 6–1).

EXTENDING COVERAGE

State and local governments have never been required to participate in Social Security. Initially, legal experts doubted whether the
Constitution permitted the federal government to force their participation. Although most experts now believe such power exists, the
federal government has not exercised it. About one-fourth of state
and local government employees remain outside Social Security. Most
are covered by pension plans that provide benefits similar to those
offered under Social Security or defined-benefit private employer pension plans.[17]

Extending Social Security coverage to all state and local workers
is desirable for several reasons. Most eventually earn eligibility for
Social Security through work in covered employment before, during,
or after their service as state or local government employees or as the
spouse of a covered worker. Extending coverage to currently uncovered
state and local government employees would eliminate certain gaps in
disability insurance coverage, extend survivor benefits to their spouses, and provide more retirees inflation-proof pensions based on career
earnings. Bringing into Social Security all newly hired workers in states
and localities now outside the system would reduce the projected long-
term deficit by 12 percent.[18]

TAXATION OF BENEFITS

Over half a century ago, the Internal Revenue Service quite
incomprehensibly ruled that Social Security benefits were a gratuity
that was exempt from the income tax. The vast majority of policy
experts came to regard this ruling as an aberration, but the Treasury
Department refused to reverse itself without congressional action,
which did not come until 1983. In that year, legislation directed that
up to half of Social Security benefits would be included in income
subject to tax, but only for couples and individuals with incomes
over $32,000 and $25,000, respectively. In 1993, Congress raised
the portion of benefits subject to income tax to 85 percent, but only
to the extent that individual income exceeded $34,000 and couples'
income exceeded $44,000. Even now, however, the tax system treats
Social Security benefits more favorably than it does contributory private pensions.

The general tax rule for contributory private pensions is straightforward. The part of a pension that returns contributions made from previously taxed income is exempt from further taxation. The rest of the pension is included in income subject to tax. If this rule were applied to Social Security, benefits that reflected the payroll taxes paid by workers would be free from taxation because workers cannot deduct their payroll taxes in computing personal income tax, but the rest of the Social Security benefit would be subject to taxation. For most retirees, this portion amounts to at least 85 percent of their benefits. Applying these rules to Social Security would close 21 percent of the projected long-term Social Security deficit if the exemptions of $25,000 for single filers and $32,000 for couples were repealed and 7 percent if they were retained.

While the income tax revenues generated by taxing all other income sources are regarded as general revenues, those attributable to taxing Social Security benefits are earmarked for the Social Security and Medicare trust funds. Social Security's share reached $9.1 billion in 1998 and would have been $25.5 billion higher if the tax rules for private pensions had been applied to Social Security and the income thresholds were removed. This policy is really a back-door way of funneling general revenues into support for Social Security. Given the history of restricting Social Security investments to low-yielding Treasury securities, such a back-door general revenue transfer to the trust funds is justified.

INVESTMENT OF RESERVES

From Social Security's inception, its reserves could be invested only in securities guaranteed as to principal and interest by the federal government. Most trust fund holdings consist of special nonmarketable securities that carry the average interest rate of Treasury securities that mature in four or more years and are outstanding at the time the special securities are issued. These special issues can be sold back to the Treasury at par at any time—a feature not available on publicly held notes and bonds. In contrast, the market prices of ordinary government bonds fluctuate before they mature. By preventing the trust funds from trading these special issues in the open market, Congress eliminated the possibility that trust fund sales might be seen as depressing prices of government bonds, thereby causing losses to private investors holding the same issues. That policymakers viewed government securities as the only appropriate investment for workers' retirement funds in the midst of the Great Depression is not surprising. The stock market collapse and widespread corporate bond defaults were vivid in people's memories.

Legislation enacted in 1977 moved Social Security from pay-as-you-go financing to "partial reserve financing" with the accumulation of significant reserves. Poor economic performance prevented these reserves from materializing. Further legislation in 1983, together with improved economic performance, led subsequently to the steady growth of reserves. At the end of 1998, reserves totaled close to $760 billion, roughly twice annual benefits. Under current policy, these reserves are projected to grow to over $2.5 trillion by 2010, about 3.4 times annual benefits. Measures adopted to close the projected long-run deficit in Social Security may well produce much larger reserves. As reserves grow, the loss of income to Social Security from restricting its investment to relatively low-yielding special Treasury issues also increases.

Why Not Private Securities? While Congress forbade the trust funds from being invested in private stocks or bonds in part because the trust funds' managers might have to sell at a loss and such sales could depress values of assets also held in private portfolios, an even more important consideration was the fear that political pressures might lead the trust funds' managers to interfere with private business decisions. Federal Reserve chairman Alan Greenspan echoed these fears in 1998. Prohibiting investments in private securities of any kind solved this problem in the simplest possible way.

Such a restriction, however, has unfortunate consequences. It denies Social Security beneficiaries the full returns that investment in a diversified portfolio generates. To the extent that the trust funds' reserve accumulation adds to national saving, it generates total returns for the nation equal to the average return on *private* investment, which averages about 6 to 7 percent more than the rate of inflation. However, investments in government securities are projected to earn only 2.8 percent more than inflation over the next seventy-five years. Forcing Social Security to invest only in low-yielding assets raises the payroll tax rate necessary to sustain any given level of benefits. Conversely, for any given tax rate, investment restrictions lower the benefits pensioners will receive. This loss falls particularly hard on the majority of retirees who derive most of their incomes from Social Security.

The practical question is how to avoid these disadvantages. Three ways exist—each with its own shortcomings. We examined one—privatization—in detail in the previous chapter. It permits holders of personal retirement accounts to make diversified investments that may earn higher returns. Unfortunately, privatization also forces individual workers to shoulder risks they are ill-equipped to bear and, under some variants, generates large and wasteful administrative expenses. Two other changes to the current system would bring workers the benefits of diversified investments while preserving the benefit security and low administrative costs of Social Security.

General Revenues. The first and simplest option would be to use general revenues to compensate the trust funds for the reduced yield resulting from investment restrictions. Congress could compensate the trust funds by transferring sums annually to make up the difference between the estimated total return to investment financed by the trust funds' saving and the yield on government bonds. The transfer required to make up the shortfall in 1998, when the trust funds' average balance was approximately $706 billion, would have been $23 billion, more than two and one-half times the amount that is transferred to the trust funds from income taxes on benefits.[19] Additional transfers would be necessary to compensate the trust funds for past revenue losses.

General revenue transfers to social insurance plans are commonplace around the world. They provide one-fifth or more of revenues for retirement pensions in Australia, Denmark, Germany, Japan, New Zealand, and Switzerland. Many early supporters proposed that one-third of Social Security revenue should come from general revenues, and some attacked the actual system because it relied exclusively on payroll taxes. Nevertheless, this simplest of ways to compensate Social Security taxpayers and beneficiaries for the restrictions placed on the trust funds' investments would be strongly opposed by many.[20] Some would object to the tax increases or spending cuts needed to finance the general revenue transfer. Others would argue that general revenue financing would weaken the program's social insurance rationale through which payroll tax contributions create an "earned right" to benefits.

Direct Investments in Private Securities. Some policymakers and analysts have concluded that part of the trust funds' reserves should be invested in private stocks and bonds. But these proposals have met criticism on both economic and political grounds. Merely shifting the trust funds' investments from government to private securities would not directly affect national saving, investment, the capital stock, or production. The trust funds would earn higher returns because they would hold assets other than relatively low-yielding government bonds. Private savers would earn somewhat lower returns because their portfolios would contain fewer common stocks and more government bonds—those that the trust funds no longer purchased. But the net effect of a shift in the trust funds' investment policy vestment, and trade might occur if private savers changed their demand for foreign assets. Furthermore, government borrowing rates might have to rise a bit to induce private investors to buy the bonds that the trust funds no longer held. With $3.8 trillion in outstanding debt, an increase of borrowing costs by ten basis points (0.1 percentage points) would raise annual federal debt service costs by $3.8 billion. There is also the complication that champions of other trust funds—including those held for Medicare hospital insurance, unemployment compensation, airports, and highways—would probably seek authorization to invest their trust fund balances in higher yielding assets.

The political question, which has troubled Congress since the inception of Social Security, concerns the possibility that the trust funds' investments in private securities might lead to inappropriate government influence over private companies. Private and state government pension funds sometimes vote their shares to change the policies of companies whose shares they own. The fear is that Social Security trustees might be subject to political pressures that force them to sell shares in companies making products some people regard as noxious (for example, cigarettes or napalm) or that pursue business practices some people regard as objectionable (such as hiring children, paying very low wages in other countries, polluting, or not providing health insurance for their workers). Alternatively, the critics fear that the trust funds would retain shares in such companies and use stockholder voting power to try to exercise control over private companies.

If these fears had substance, we would join those who oppose such investments, regardless of the income loss to pensioners. A good deal of experience shows that these concerns are exaggerated, however. Several government trust funds now invest in private securities. Managers of the Thrift Savings Plan for government workers and the pension plans of the Federal Reserve Board, the U.S. Air Force, and the Tennessee Valley Authority have not exercised any control over the companies in which they invest and have pursued only financial objectives in selecting portfolios (see Box 6–4, page 112).

This experience indicates that similar arrangements could also protect Social Security trustees from succumbing to political pressures. Nonetheless, we propose additional institutional safeguards that would make it impossible, as a practical matter, to use the trust funds' reserves to influence corporate policy.

The Social Security Reserve Board. Certain organizational reforms could all but eliminate the risk of political interference with investment decisions by Social Security trustees. Management of Social Security reserves could be placed in the hands of an independent board—the Social Security Reserve Board (SSRB)—modeled after the Federal Reserve Board. The Federal Reserve system performs two politically charged tasks: controlling growth of the money supply and regulating private banks. Despite the political sensitivity of these issues, the Federal Reserve system has sustained its political independence for eight decades. Federal Reserve governors are appointed by the president and confirmed by the Senate, serve staggered fourteen-year terms, and cannot be removed for political reasons. Members of the SSRB would be appointed with similar protections.

To manage the trust funds' reserves, the power of the SSRB would be limited to selecting fund managers on the basis of competitive bids. The fund managers would be authorized only to make passive investments in securities—bonds or stocks—of companies chosen to represent broad market indexes. These investments would have to be merged with funds managed on behalf of private account holders. To prevent the SSRB or its fund managers from exercising any voice in management of private companies and SSRB share ownership from diluting control of private shareholders, Congress could insist on either of two precautions. It could eliminate voting rights on shares held by the SSRB. Or it could employ a number of fund managers, so that total shares voted by each manager would be less than a target proportion of outstanding stock of any company—say 1 percent.

BOX 6–4
FEDERAL INVESTMENT IN PRIVATE SECURITIES

All federal employees hired since 1984 are covered by the Federal Employees Retirement System (FERS) and have the option of participating in the Thrift Savings Plan (TSP). TSP now gives participants the option of contributing to three index funds: a government securities investment (G) fund; a common stock index investment (C) fund; and a fixed income investment (F) fund. The managers plan to add two other funds originally authorized by Congress—a small-capitalization stock index (S) fund and an international stock index (I) fund.

The TSP had 2.3 million individual accounts in mid-1998. Assets totaled over $66 billion and were growing at $500 million a month. Administrative costs varied from 8 to 10 basis points. Participants in FERS receive an automatic contribution to their TSP accounts from their employing agency equal to 1 percent of their basic pay. Employees can contribute up to 10 percent of their salary on a pretax basis. Their agencies match the first 3 percentage points of these contributions on a dollar-for-dollar basis and the next 2 percentage points on a $1-for-every-$2 basis.

The Federal Retirement Thrift Investment Board, which manages the three funds, consists of an executive director and five members appointed by the president. To minimize chances of political interference, the G fund is invested exclusively in short-term, nonmarketable special Treasury issues, the F fund is invested in an index mutual fund that tracks the Lehman Brothers Aggregate bond index, and the C fund in an equity mutual fund that tracks the Standard and Poor's 500 stock index. The C and F funds are managed under contract by the largest private manager of index funds in the United States.

Congress explicitly considered whether to model the TSP on individual retirement accounts, which permit account holders to select among a broad menu of private stocks and funds, but opted instead on centralized management. It stated its reasons in the *Congressional Record* (H.R. Rep. No. 99–606, pp. 137–38):

> As an alternative the committee considered permitting any qualified institution to offer [employees] specific investment vehicles. However, the committee rejected that approach for a number of reasons. First, there are literally thousands of qualified institutions who would bombard employees with promotions for their services. The committee concluded that employees would not favor such an approach. Second, few, if any, private employers offer such an arrangement. Third, even qualified institutions go bankrupt occasionally and a substantial portion of an employee's retirement benefit could be wiped out. This is in contrast to the diversified fund approach, which could easily survive a few bankruptcies. Fourth, it would be difficult to administer. Fifth, this "retail" or "voucher" approach would give up the economic advantage of this group's wholesale purchasing power derived from its large size, so that employees acting individually would get less for their money.

Furthermore, fund managers would be required by law to vote shares solely in the economic interest of future beneficiaries.

This system would triply insulate fund management from political control by elected officials. Long-term appointments and security of tenure would protect the SSRB from political interference. Limitation of investments to passively managed funds and pooling with private accounts would prevent the SSRB from exercising power by selecting shares. The elimination or diffusion of voting rights among independent fund managers would prevent the SSRB from using voting power to influence company management and would protect voting rights of private shareholders from dilution. Congress and the president would have no effective way to influence private companies through the trust funds unless they revamped the SSRB structure. While nothing other than a constitutional amendment can prevent Congress from repealing a previously enacted law, the political costs of doing so would be high. Furthermore, when Congress feels the urge to influence the policies of private businesses, it has many far more powerful and direct instruments to accomplish those ends than through management of the Social Security trust funds. The federal government can tax, regulate, or subsidize private companies to encourage or force them to engage in or desist from particular policies. No private company or lower level of government has similar powers.

It is important to note that private retirement accounts are not immune to political control. Congress could stipulate that savings in tax-sheltered accounts will not qualify for favored tax treatment if investments do not meet certain federally established requirements— such as directing a certain portion of funds to stipulated social objectives or avoiding investments in companies that carry out objectionable policies. Congress could also deny tax advantages to funds that act contrary to public policy. Such regulations would be politically viable only under extraordinary conditions, but these conditions would be no more extraordinary than those under which the procedural safeguards we have outlined for Social Security could be breached.

With these institutional safeguards in place, we recommend that Social Security reserves be partly invested in a broad mix of private securities. Any steps in this direction should proceed gradually and be monitored carefully. A contingency reserve fund equal to one and one-half year's benefits should be held in special Treasury securities. Half of total reserves would be invested gradually over the next decade or two in a mix of equities that reflected a broad index of domestic stocks. The balance in excess of the contingency fund would be invested in an index of corporate bonds. This more diversified investment policy would close some 69 percent of the projected long-term deficit when combined with the other reforms we have described.[21]

MAINTAINING FUNDING

Under the economic and demographic assumptions now used to evaluate the long-run solvency of Social Security, the measures we have recommended are sufficient to generate large and growing Social Security surpluses, not just over the next seventy-five years but indefinitely. Of course, economic and demographic developments will not unfold precisely as current projections assume. Today's best guesses about the future will prove to be inaccurate, making future adjustments in benefits or taxes necessary to sustain long-run balance or forestall excessive surpluses. Policymakers have tended to procrastinate when the required adjustments involve imposing pain on beneficiaries or taxpayers. For this reason, an automatic adjustment mechanism should be part of a strengthened and modernized Social Security program. Specifically, should revenues and reserves fall 5 percent or more below expenditures projected over the next seventy-five years, Congress should enact legislation requiring it to consider, under expedited procedures, legislation to correct the imbalance. If Congress failed to act within a set period—say, one year from notification—automatic tax increases and benefit cuts would take effect, each sufficient to close half of the projected deficit.

CONCLUSION

We have described changes in Social Security sufficient to convert the projected long-term deficit into a projected surplus. Most of the items call for modest benefit cuts, but we also propose increased benefits for widows and widowers. Although our menu includes an increase in the portion of benefits subject to tax, no tax increase is needed to restore long-term balance. Most importantly, the menu closes the projected long-term deficit with room to spare. It does so without modifying the

basic structure and key strengths of the current Social Security system—
the defined-benefit pension structure, which protects workers from
financial market and other risks to their safety-net income; the social
assistance to low earners, strengthened by improved protection of widows; and full adjustment for correctly measured inflation.

These reforms would also build and maintain a larger trust fund
to raise national saving, provided that future Congresses and presidents do not use the program's surpluses to mask deficits in the other
operations of government or justify benefit increases or tax cuts in
Social Security.

The budget history of the past decade gives some reason for opti-
mism. As Social Security reserves have risen from less than three
months of benefit payments in 1985 to twenty-two months of benefit payments at the end of 1998, Congress has cut deficits on other
operations of government. The growth of Social Security reserves did
not derail the deficit reduction programs enacted in 1990, 1993, and
1997, which, along with economic growth, reduced the deficit on
operations of government other than Social Security from 5.4 percent of GDP in 1985 to 0.5 percent of GDP in 1998.

The real test, however, began in 1998. Unified budget surpluses
emerged for the first time in twenty-nine years. The budget, exclud-
ing Social Security, is projected to reach balance early in the next
decade and to show growing surpluses for at least fifteen years thereafter. In this environment, we think additional procedural reforms
could help assure that the trust funds' surpluses fulfill their economic function of boosting national saving. If Social Security reserves are
invested in private securities, as we urge, such safeguards would be
even more important. If asset prices were to rise faster than assumed
in the actuarial projections, Social Security might appear to be over-
funded. Elected officials might well rush to use this windfall for politically popular benefit increases or tax cuts. Should asset prices
subsequently decline, we fear that elected officials would be loath to
cut benefits or raise taxes.

We propose that Congress enact targets for trust fund accumulation similar in general structure to those it has established for private
defined-benefit pension funds under the Employee Retirement Income
Security Act. Furthermore, the Social Security Reserve Board should
be required to evaluate all proposed changes to Social Security benefits and taxes to determine if the legislation would retard achievement of these targets. If the SSRB judged that the proposed legislation

would reduce the trust funds' balance over a five-, ten-, or seventy-five-year period, a super majority vote would be required for Senate passage.[22] In the House of Representatives, no similar restraint is possible because a majority vote determines the rules under which each piece of legislation is considered. Even in the House, however, a negative report from the SSRB would inhibit legislation that would jeopardize the financial soundness of Social Security.

In addition, the operations of Social Security, which are now officially "off-budget," should be removed from the main budget totals reported by the Office of Management and Budget and the Congressional Budget Office. Budget resolutions enacted annually to guide congressional action should exclude Social Security from aggregate totals. Administrative changes could add substance to the 1994 legislation that made the Social Security Administration an independent agency and separated Social Security from other operations of government.[23]

7

PROPOSALS TO REFORM SOCIAL SECURITY: A REPORT CARD

Policy makers and the public face a bewildering array of proposals to reform or replace Social Security. Members of Congress, business organizations, academicians, and think tanks have produced dozens of proposals. The 1994–96 Advisory Council on Social Security alone developed three different plans, none of which won majority support.

Fortunately for the interested citizen, almost all proposals fall into one of three categories: plans to replace the current system entirely with private accounts, plans to replace the current system partly with private accounts, or plans to strengthen and modernize the current system. There are two other approaches to Social Security reform—making retirement saving strictly voluntary and imposing means or income tests as a condition for benefits—but few have developed detailed plans along such lines. Moreover, for the reasons we describe in Boxes 3–6 and 7–1 (see page 118), we consider these approaches both ill considered and unworkable.

In this chapter, we propose four criteria for evaluating reform plans. We apply these criteria to several plans that exemplify the three major approaches to reform and grade these plans from A to D.[1] We give no plan a failing grade of F because all would restore financial balance to the nation's basic retirement system. A grade of D means

Box 7–1
Why Means Testing of Social
Security Doesn't Make Sense

Peter G. Peterson, former secretary of Commerce, has proposed that all federal benefits to individuals, including Social Security and Medicare, be subject to an affluence test.[a] Under this plan, which has been endorsed by the Concord Coalition, households with incomes at least $5,000 over the national median would have their benefits scaled back 1 percent for each $1,000 by which their annual income including benefits exceeded the threshold. In other words, a household with an income $30,000 above the threshold would have its benefits scaled back 30 percent. The maximum amount by which benefits could be reduced would be 85 percent.

This approach seeks to lower benefits most for those who need them least. This same principle is reflected in the current Social Security benefit formula, which provides higher replacement rates for workers with low average earnings than for workers with high average earnings. It also is the logic behind the progressive income tax.

Unfortunately, this principle would have undesirable consequences if applied to Social Security benefits. It would increase penalties on work and saving, raise insurmountable administrative problems, and undermine the basic rationale of Social Security.

To see how the affluence test would work if applied to income—and the problems it would generate—consider a retired wife receiving $10,000 a year in Social Security and her working husband who earns $30,000 a year. They also receive $25,000 in income from their investments. Given median income of $32,000 in 1997, the affluence test would reduce the retiree's Social Security by $2,800. If the retiree's husband stopped working, she would not suffer this benefit reduction. They could also avoid the affluence test in whole or in part if they shifted their investments into assets that generated little income, but promised subsequent capital gains.

These responses, which would undermine the intent of an income test, could be minimized if the test were applied to net worth, rather than annual income. Unfortunately, net worth tests are even more costly to administer than income tests, as they require annual valuations of all assets, many of which are not generally traded. Furthermore, asset tests are easily evaded now that the financial market is global.

An income test violates the fundamental political compact that underlies Social Security— that a lifetime of work in jobs requiring payment of the payroll tax entitles a worker to a benefit based on average earnings when that worker reaches retirement age. Without this principle, there would be no rationale for financing benefits with a payroll tax or relating benefits to past earnings. An income test upsets this principle by denying benefits, regardless of earnings or payroll taxes paid, to people who saved a lot, had earnings, were lucky in investments, or were blessed by significant inheritance. The principle of relating benefits to past earnings is not sacrosanct. But introducing an income or asset test would erode the political basis for payroll tax-supported social insurance.

---

a. Peter G. Peterson, *Will America Grow Up Before It Grows Old?* (New York: Random House, 1996), and *Facing Up: How to Rescue the Economy from Crushing Debt and Restore the American Dream* (New York: Simon and Schuster, 1993).

that we regard a plan as so severely flawed that it does not merit serious consideration. A grade of C means that a plan contains major shortcomings according to the criteria we propose. A grade of B means that a plan has significant strengths and meets most requirements for reform, but comes up short in one or more key respects. The grade of A means that a plan meets all major requirements for reform and falls seriously short in none. Not everyone will agree with our evaluations. Some may object to the particular criteria we have selected or the importance we attach to them. Others may think we have been too harsh or lenient in grading a particular plan. In the end, you must form your own judgment.

CRITERIA FOR REFORM

Our first criterion requires that a good reform plan ensure *adequate* benefits that are *equitably* distributed and represent a *fair return* for taxes paid. Current benefits are not unduly generous, as we showed in Box 6–1. For that reason, *adequacy* means that large benefit cuts are unacceptable because they would result in insufficient protection for retirees, the disabled, and survivors. Overall benefit increases are also undesirable because they would further swell the added costs the retiring baby boomers will generate. *Equity* requires that protection be maintained for low earners, large families, and other vulnerable people. And a *fair return* means that plans should be invested wisely and not incur needless administrative costs.

Our second criterion is that the unavoidable *risks of long-term pension commitments should be shared broadly*, not placed on the shoulders of individual workers. Our third criterion for judging plans is *administrative efficiency and feasibility*. In addition to avoiding needless administrative costs, the plan should not be unduly complex for private businesses, workers, and the government. Finally, we give higher grades to plans that *raise national saving*. A plan's contribution to national saving is determined by its additions to reserves held in either the trust funds or individual accounts, less any induced reductions that take place in private saving or government surpluses outside the retirement system.

Other consequences of Social Security reform are also important. How reform will influence retirement decisions, for example, will be of increasing importance as labor force growth slows to a crawl during the first decades of the twenty-first century. Reform may also change the relative treatment of one- and two-earner couples, a subject of particular concern to the growing number of working women. While these—and many other—dimensions of reform are of concern, no plan that provides inadequate benefits, fails to protect low earners, and gives a poor return for each dollar of taxes paid; that subjects workers to excessive risk; that generates needless administrative complexity; and that does nothing to boost national saving should merit serious consideration. (See the appendix to this chapter, page 141, and Table 7–1, for some specifics about the major plans.)

PROPOSALS TO REPLACE SOCIAL SECURITY

Several plans would replace Social Security with a wholly new system based on personal retirement accounts. The plans differ in how much assistance they would give low earners beyond the accumulation in each worker's personal account, how much discretion individuals would have to select investments for their accounts, how much control participants would have over the way benefits are paid from their personal accounts when they retire, how much risk individual workers would face, how the plans would be administered, and how the costs of transition to the new system would be paid for.

PERSONAL SECURITY ACCOUNT PLAN

The Personal Security Account plan, advanced by five members of the 1994–96 Advisory Council on Social Security, would gradually replace Social Security with two other benefits, one based on balances accumulated in mandated IRA-like personal retirement accounts, the other a flat annuity based on how long the recipient had worked and the age at which benefits were first received.

The plan would be phased in over many years. Workers under age 25 when the new plan came into effect would receive benefits only under the new system. Workers between the ages of 25 and 55 would receive a blend of benefits under the new and old systems. Retirees and workers over age 55 would remain under the current

TABLE 7-1
POLICIES TO REFORM SOCIAL SECURITY AND REDUCE THE LONG-TERM DEFICIT CONTAINED IN SEVEN SOCIAL SECURITY REFORM PLANS

	PERSONAL SECURITY ACCOUNT	FELDSTEIN	INDIVIDUAL ACCOUNT	MOYNIHAN	BREAUX-GREGG	BALL	MAINTAIN STRUCTURE
BENEFIT REDUCTIONS							
1. Accelerate to 2011 the scheduled increase to 67 in age at which unreduced benefits are available	X		X	X	X		X
2. Increase age at which unreduced benefits are available to 68 by 2017 (*to 70 by 2029)				X	X*		
3. After 1 or 2 above, increase age at which unreduced benefits are available to keep the fraction of adult life in retirement constant (*by one month every two years, ** by one month every year and a half)	X		X	X*	X**		X
4. Increase age of initial eligibility along with age at which unreduced benefits are available	X				X		X
5. Reduce spouse's benefit to one-third of worker's benefit			X		X		X
6. Average earnings over thirty-eight (*forty years) rather than thirty-five years when computing benefits			X	X	X*	X	X
7. Reduce replacement rate for those with higher average earnings			X		X		
8. Reduce disability benefits	X		X		X		
9. Reduce annual cost-of-living adjustment				X	X		

Continued on next page

TABLE 7–1 (CONT'D.)

	Personal Security Account	Feldstein	Individual Account	Moynihan	Breaux-Gregg	Ball	Maintain Structure
BENEFIT ENHANCEMENTS							
10. Eliminate earnings test (* at the normal retirement age)	X			X	X*		
11. Raise benefits for surviving spouse to 75 percent of the couple's combined benefit			X				X
12. Ease disability requirements for those affected by the increase in the age of initial benefit eligibility							X
REVENUE INCREASES							
13. Subject more of benefits to the income tax	X		X	X		X	X
14. Raise payroll tax rates (*lower rates initially followed by higher rates)	X		X	X*			
15. Raise maximum earnings subject to payroll tax				X		X	
16. Borrow from the public or channel general revenues into retirement accounts	X	X			X		
OTHER							
17. Establish individual retirement accounts (* voluntary)	X	X	X	X*	X		
18. Require all new state and local employees to join Social Security	X		X	X	X	X	X
19. Establish minimum non-earnings-related benefit	X				X		
20. Invest the trust funds' reserves in private, as well as government assets						X	X

Social Security system. No retiree would receive benefits entirely under the new system for about forty years. Payroll tax rates would be increased 1.52 percentage points until virtually all adults now alive are either dead or retired—that is, for about seven decades, a period the architects designate "the transition." The added tax is needed because continued Social Security benefits for current retirees and older workers, the new flat pension, and deposits into personal accounts would cost more than the current 12.4 percent payroll tax will generate. Even with the tax increase, the new system would run a deficit for the first few decades, forcing the government to borrow approximately $2 trillion (in 1998 dollars). Eventually, as Social Security phases out, revenues would exceed costs and the debt would be paid off. When all the initial borrowing had been repaid—around the year 2070—the supplemental payroll tax could be repealed.

The Personal Security Account plan has other important implications. The first-tier flat benefit would guarantee inflation-protected payments until the worker and his or her spouse died. The second-tier benefit would not provide protection against inflation or a long life unless the worker chose to purchase an inflation-indexed annuity with his or her personal account balance. All of the flat benefit, but none of the pension provided from the personal accounts, would be included in income subject to the income tax. Relative to current rules, this feature would raise taxes on low- and moderate-income retirees and decrease them on higher-income retirees. The Personal Security Account plan would retain the disability insurance program but would gradually cut benefits. Furthermore, the disabled would not have access to their personal retirement account until they reach retirement age. Even then, the balances of those who became disabled when young and made deposits for only a few years would be small. Workers would enjoy control over investment and withdrawal of their retirement funds, but would sacrifice reliability and face sharply higher administrative costs.

Benefit Adequacy and Equity. While the plan promises good benefits for retirees on the average, it provides poor protection to certain vulnerable groups. It cuts disability benefits as much as 30 percent. Divorcees who earned little during their married years, possibly because they were busy raising children, could find themselves with little more than the flat benefit. Because the Personal Security

Account plan would permit workers to invest their individual accounts in quite different portfolios, some workers would do poorly and, therefore, have to depend on the flat benefit for the bulk of their retirement income.

Protection against Risk. The pension provided through the flat benefit—an inflation-adjusted annuity—would provide reliable protection against risk. That derived from the personal accounts, however, would expose retirees to considerable uncertainty. Pensions for workers with similar earnings would vary widely because returns on personal accounts would depend on how funds were invested, what administrative fees were imposed by fund managers, how high asset values were when balances were withdrawn, and whether pensioners bought annuities when they retired. Those who invested unwisely, had bad luck, or spent their accumulated savings too fast could find themselves dependent, in their later years, on the plan's flat benefit.

Administrative Efficiency. The Personal Security Account plan does poorly on this criterion. The administrative structure for the current Social Security system would have to be maintained for many years. In addition, the tax collection and record-keeping systems needed for payment of survivor and disability benefits would continue and a simplified system would have to be established to administer the flat benefit. Another new structure would be required to ensure that employers made timely and accurate deposits into personal accounts and that the financial institutions managing personal accounts complied with the inevitable regulations. The administrative burdens imposed on small employers would be so burdensome that we doubt that the plan could actually function as envisioned. Even large employers would find it onerous to direct periodic deposits—many of which would be less than $100 a month—to the numerous fund managers chosen by their employees.

On average, workers would face dramatically higher administrative costs that would seriously lower the net returns to workers, compared to plans that managed similar investments centrally. Since some of these costs do not vary with the size of accounts, they would represent a larger portion of income of small accounts than on large accounts.[2] Furthermore, those pensioners who wished to buy annuities would face large additional costs.

National Saving. The Personal Security Account plan ranks relatively high on adding to national saving because it raises payroll taxes. However, the personal accounts would be so similar to existing IRAs and 401(k) plans that workers would probably reduce other private saving more than if the accounts were held and managed centrally by the government. Furthermore, if experience with IRAs is any indication, Congress would come under pressure to allow withdrawals from personal accounts for specified meritorious uses well before retirement. Such withdrawals would reduce the resources available to support retirement pensions and any positive effect on national saving. A similar problem would arise with all individual account plans, but it is most serious for plans that set up accounts similar to current tax-sheltered savings arrangements.

Overall, we give the Personal Security Account plan a grade of C (see Table 7–2).

TABLE 7–2
REPORT CARD FOR THE
PERSONAL SECURITY ACCOUNT PLAN

CRITERIA	GRADE
Adequacy, equity, and a fair return	C +
Protection against risk	C
Administrative efficiency	D
Increased national saving	B
Overall grade	C

FELDSTEIN PLAN

Under a plan crafted by Martin Feldstein, professor of economics at Harvard University and a former chairman of the Council of Economic Advisers, each worker would deposit 2 percent of his or her earnings, up to the maximum subject to the payroll tax, in a personal retirement account.[3] Workers would receive an income tax credit sufficient to offset the cost of these deposits. For those with no tax liability or liabilities less than 2 percent of earnings, the tax credit would be refundable. For as long as they last, the projected budget surpluses would be used to finance the tax credits. Increased federal borrowing, tax increases, or spending cuts would then be required for a number of years.

The personal retirement accounts, which would represent a massive infusion of new resources into the mandatory retirement system, would be invested in regulated stock and bond funds chosen by the worker and administered by private fund managers. When workers reached retirement age and began to draw pensions from their personal retirement accounts, their Social Security benefits would be reduced by $3 for every $4 withdrawn. In effect, the benefits promised by the current Social Security program would become a floor under pensions. Overall, retirees would receive an estimated 60 percent of their benefits from Social Security and 40 percent from their personal accounts. Higher earners would depend more on their personal accounts than these averages suggest, and some would receive nothing from Social Security. The reductions in Social Security benefits would eventually be sufficient to close the projected long-term Social Security deficit.

Benefit Adequacy and Equity. This plan would raise, not lower, the baby boomers' pensions. Given widespread concern about the projected costs of supporting pension and medical benefits for the elderly and disabled, we regard proposals to raise benefits as imprudent. The Feldstein plan would provide larger retirement benefits than those of any other plan we examine, larger in fact than those promised by the current Social Security system. More generous benefits are possible because the plan uses the budget surpluses projected for the next two decades to support deposits into individual accounts.[4] When these surpluses begin to shrink, taxes dedicated to retirement pensions will have to be raised, other spending cut, or deficits incurred for several decades.

The benefit increases would be inequitably distributed. Benefits would rise proportionately more for high earners than for low earners. The contribution to individual accounts and, hence, the size of account balances would be a constant fraction of income. Social Security benefits are proportionately larger for low earners than for high earners. Since the plan would reduce Social Security benefits by three-quarters of any benefits derived from individual accounts, pensions for high earners would rise proportionately more than would pensions of low earners. The following simple numerical example, which is presented in monthly amounts, illustrates this point.

	AVERAGE EARNINGS	SOCIAL SECURITY	INDIVIDUAL ACCOUNT	TOTAL PENSION	CHANGE IN PENSION
Low Earner	$1,000	$560	$240	$620	+11%
High Earner	$5,600	$1,375	$1,340	$1,720	+25%

The Social Security benefits in the table correspond approximately to the replacement rates of low and maximum earners—56 percent and 25 percent respectively. Each worker contributes proportionately to individual accounts and, therefore, receives a pension proportionate to earnings. When Social Security benefits are reduced by three-quarters of the pension based on the individual account, the low earner's total pension goes up 11 percent, the high earner's by 25 percent. Since high earners are likely to select higher-yielding, albeit riskier, portfolios, the increase in benefits for higher earners relative to that for low earners is likely to be even larger than this illustration shows. In short, high earners would tend to receive little from Social Security and, in the extreme case, might receive nothing.

Protection against Risk. At the level of the individual pensioner, the Feldstein plan provides substantial protection against market risk because it guarantees participants a pension at least as large as that promised by the current benefit formula. However, the plan is likely to undermine political support for a defined-benefit guarantee like Social Security among high and moderate earners because most of them would eventually receive pensions based predominantly on their personal accounts. We explore this issue in more detail in the next chapter. Furthermore, the plan poses major fiscal risks because the commitment to increased pensions would generate severe budget pressures, particularly after currently projected budget surpluses end. The fiscal duress would affect all government spending and taxes.

Administrative Efficiency. The Feldstein plan would be complex and costly to administer. As was true with the Personal Security Account plan, administrative and investment management fees will eat into returns on personal retirement account balances. The IRS would face numerous problems when it tried to refund the tax credit to those with no or limited tax liabilities. Nor would it be easy for the Social Security Administration to design and operate a system that reduced Social Security benefits by $3 for every $4 withdrawn from each retiree's personal account.[5]

National Saving. The effects of the Feldstein plan on national saving are complicated and unclear.[6] Initially, the plan would not affect saving at all, as the deposits in individual accounts would simply substitute for the reduction in federal debt that will occur if the projected budget surpluses are not dissipated through tax cuts or spending increases. The longer-run effects on saving depend on how successive Congresses and presidents react when the surpluses are no longer large enough to sustain the required deposits into the individual accounts and on the extent to which individuals cut back on other saving to offset mandatory saving in individual accounts.

The Feldstein plan deserves the same overall grade that was given to the Personal Security Account plan (see Table 7–3).

TABLE 7–3
REPORT CARD FOR THE FELDSTEIN PLAN

CRITERIA	GRADE
Adequacy, equity, and a fair return	B +
Protection against risk	B-
Administrative efficiency	D-
Increased national saving	D
Overall grade	C

REDUCE SOCIAL SECURITY AND SUPPLEMENT IT WITH SMALL PERSONAL ACCOUNTS

Another group of proposals would supplement a reduced Social Security system with small defined-contribution personal retirement accounts. These plans would scale back defined-benefit Social Security pensions by different amounts and in different ways, and would create personal retirement accounts of various sizes and forms.

INDIVIDUAL ACCOUNT PLAN

The Individual Account plan, crafted by Edward M. Gramlich, chairman of the 1994–96 Advisory Council on Social Security, would cut back Social Security outlays sufficiently so that the current 12.4 percent payroll tax would cover future program costs. Benefits relative to those promised under current law would be cut gradually—by little for low earners and up to more than 25 percent for high earners (see the appendix to this chapter, pages 142–43, and Table 7-1 for details). An increase in the *employee* payroll tax by 1.6 percentage points would finance small personal retirement accounts invested in a restricted number of index mutual funds managed by a government agency. Balances would be converted into inflation-protected annuities when workers reach retirement age.

The annuities would be small. A worker with median covered earnings who was 40 years old when the plan was implemented would receive an annuity of about $125 (in 1998 dollars) a month starting at age 65, which would equal about 13 percent of the worker's expected Social Security benefit under the current system.[7] Older workers, who would start contributing at a later age, would contribute for fewer years and would receive less; younger workers would participate for more years and receive larger pensions. Because payroll taxes would fully finance the new individual accounts, the plan would require no other transitional taxes or borrowing. However, the Individual Account plan would cut disability benefits by varying amounts depending on earnings. As with the Personal Security Account plan, individual accounts can do nothing to offset these cuts until the disabled reach retirement age, and not much even then for workers who become disabled when young.

Benefit Adequacy and Equity. Despite its name, the Individual Account plan would continue to rely heavily on Social Security, although benefits provided through that program would ultimately be cut by over 25 percent for high earners. On the average, pensions financed by individual accounts would fill in this gap for people of retirement age. But the disabled would suffer reduced benefits until they reached retirement age. The cuts in the defined-benefit component of the reformed system are larger than necessary because the Individual Account plan would continue to prohibit managers of the Social Security trust funds from investing in a diversified portfolio. The adequacy of pensions based on individual accounts would vary among workers of a given age and over time, depending on their choice of index funds and market performance.

Protection against Risk. The individual accounts would be subject to market risk, but the variation would be less than that of the Personal Security Account and Feldstein plans because investments would be limited to a few centrally managed index funds. The pensions based on personal retirement accounts would never constitute more than a modest portion of future retirees' pensions—about 30 percent of the benefits for an average wage worker and 20 percent of those for a low earner. Both the pension provided through the scaled-back Social Security and that provided from the individual account would be inflation-protected annuities.

Administrative Efficiency. Administrative costs for the Individual Account plan would be somewhat higher than those under Social Security. Central administration, mandatory annuitization, and the limited number of indexed investments would hold down costs. But the federal government would have to establish arrangements for depositing funds in accounts of each worker's choice, educating them about the options, and responding to questions. It would also have to keep track of divorces if funds accumulated in personal accounts were divided at divorce, an important protection for lesser earners, usually wives, and an issue facing all plans with individual accounts.

National Saving. The increased payroll tax and the benefit cuts would both raise national saving. Workers would probably reduce their private saving less per dollar in their individual account than they would under the Personal Security Account and Feldstein plans because these centrally held accounts would not be viewed as good substitutes for IRAs or 401(k) plans, from which withdrawals under certain circumstances are permitted.

We give the Individual Account plan a solid B for an overall grade (see Table 7–4).

TABLE 7–4
REPORT CARD FOR THE
INDIVIDUAL ACCOUNT PLAN

CRITERIA	GRADE
Adequacy, equity, and a fair return	B
Protection against risk	B
Administrative efficiency	B-
Increased national saving	B+
Overall grade	B

MOYNIHAN (SOCIAL SECURITY SOLVENCY) PLAN

Senator Daniel Patrick Moynihan (Democrat of New York) proposes to cut payroll taxes, substantially lower Social Security benefits, and *authorize* workers to set up individual accounts. Payroll taxes would be cut 2 percentage points until 2025—1 percentage point for workers and 1 percentage point for employers (see the appendix to this chapter, page 145, and Table 7–1 for details). Workers would be permitted to spend or save the 1 percentage point cut in their portion of the payroll tax. They could save it either in voluntary personal accounts modeled on the Thrift Savings Plan and administered by a new government board or in special Individual Retirement Accounts managed by financial institutions of their choosing. If an employee established a personal account, the worker's employer would have to match the worker's contribution. Withdrawal of account balances at retirement would be unrestricted.

From 2025 to 2060, the payroll tax rate would be raised periodically to keep program revenues in line with benefit payments. After 2045, the combination of payroll taxes and deposits in personal accounts would exceed the current payroll tax rate. In 2060, the 13.4 percent payroll tax rate together with contributions to a personal account would claim 15.4 percent of covered earnings, 3 percentage points above the current payroll tax.

Because the Moynihan proposal would cut average payroll tax collections over the next 75 years, it would have to cut Social Security benefits more than would be necessary if taxes were maintained. Retirement, survivor, and disability benefits would be cut by an average of about 20 percent relative to current law, but the cuts would grow over time and be larger for the long-term disabled and the very old than for those who are just beginning to receive benefits. The cuts result from holding annual inflation adjustments 1 percentage point below the CPI and by cutting benefits across the board through increasing the age at which unreduced benefits are paid. Over time, the Moynihan plan would return Social Security to a pay-as-you-go system, with reserves sufficient to tide the system over a severe economic downturn.

The Moynihan plan would deny full inflation adjustments under the personal income tax and under all indexed benefit programs except Supplemental Security Income. Over time, this would cause massive increases in income tax burdens and reductions in entitlement spending for benefits for veterans, civil servants, and others.

Benefit Adequacy and Equity. This plan would erode benefits steeply and in ways that could hurt vulnerable groups the most. Those who received benefits the longest—the very old and the long-term disabled—would suffer the largest benefit reductions from the cumulative effects of the 1 percentage point reduction in the annual cost-of-living adjustment. In 2017 when the age at which unreduced benefits are paid would reach 68 under this plan, benefits for a 62-year-old retiree will be 35 percent smaller than those available at age 68. Hardship among the very old, especially widows and widowers, could increase if many are encouraged by the elimination of the earnings test for early retirees to draw these greatly reduced benefits at age 62 or 63, supplementing them with earnings while still in their 60s. When such early retirees reach their mid-70s and find even part-time work burdensome, the reduced benefits may prove inadequate, particularly for low earners, the group least likely to have set up voluntary investment accounts. The less-than-complete adjustment for inflation would only compound their difficulty.

Protection against Risk. Because workers could invest their voluntary accounts in a wide range of assets, they would be exposed to a good deal of investment risk. Social Security would provide only partial protection against inflation, and pensions derived from the voluntary accounts would have none. With no restrictions on when or how retirees could convert their account balances into retirement income, some could outlive these pensions.

Administrative Efficiency. Government administrative costs would rise because it would be necessary not only to retain the Social Security

Administration in full, but also to create a wholly new government-managed individual account system and to ensure compliance for privately managed accounts. Small and medium-sized businesses would face virtually insurmountable challenges in trying to make the program work. They would have to keep track, pay period by pay period, of whether workers (including new hires and departing workers) wanted to contribute to individual accounts or not; whether those who made contributions wanted their funds deposited in the government-managed program or in a privately administered account; and, for those who chose private accounts, which of the many thousands of private fund managers that would be vying for business the worker had selected.

National Saving. If all of its provisions remained in force, the Moynihan plan would raise national saving even though it would return to pay-as-you-go financing of Social Security. One explanation for this is that income tax collections would rise dramatically, the inevitable consequence of not indexing the tax brackets, exemptions, and the standard deduction. Another is that the growth of mandatory spending would slow because the plan would deny full inflation adjustments under all indexed benefit programs except Supplemental Security Income. If, as we think highly probable, Congress acted to preserve full inflation adjustments for the income tax system and key benefit programs, the plan would reduce national saving.

The Social Security Solvency plan developed by Senator Moynihan is inadequate and merits an overall grade no higher than a D (see Table 7–5).

TABLE 7–5
REPORT CARD FOR THE MOYNIHAN
(SOCIAL SECURITY SOLVENCY) PLAN

CRITERIA	GRADE
Adequacy, equity, and a fair return	F
Protection against risk	C+
Administrative efficiency	D-
Increased national saving	D
Overall grade	D

BREAUX-GREGG (TWENTY-FIRST CENTURY RETIREMENT) PLAN

The plan proposed by Senators John Breaux (Democrat of Louisiana), Judd Gregg (Republican of New Hampshire), and others would divert 2 percentage points of the current payroll tax to individual accounts modeled on the Thrift Savings Plan and cut Social Security benefits an average of 25 to 30 percent (see the appendix to this chapter, page 146, and Table 7–1 for details).[8] Cuts of this size would be necessary both to close the current projected long-term deficit and to free up 2 percentage points of the payroll tax for individual savings accounts. Retiring workers would be required to convert a portion of their account balances into an inflation-protected annuity. Together with the retiree's reduced Social Security benefit, this annuity would have to be sufficient to meet a standard for minimum retirement income.

Social Security benefits would be cut in four ways: by increasing the age at which unreduced benefits are available to 70 by 2029 and at a slower pace thereafter, by reducing the spouse's benefit, by shaving the cost-of-living adjustment, and by cutting replacement rates for all retirees except those with average earnings below approximately $5,700 in 1998, a threshold that would rise at the same rate as average earnings. A new minimum benefit would be established that was equal to 60 percent of the poverty threshold for those with twenty years of covered earnings, rising to 100 percent of the poverty threshold for those with forty years of earnings. A fail-safe mechanism would automatically keep the program in long-run balance and ensure that financial balance would not be jeopardized by unexpected developments.

Benefit Adequacy and Equity. The Breaux-Gregg plan, like the Individual Account plan, combines mandatory individual accounts, administered along the lines of the Thrift Savings Plan, with a scaled back Social Security system. The Breaux-Gregg plan, however, lowers both retirement and disability benefits more than the Individual Account plan does—30 to 40 percent for moderate and high earners. Larger cuts are necessary because the plan widens the program's deficit by diverting payroll taxes from Social Security, whereas the Individual Account plan raises payroll taxes to finance the personal accounts. As a consequence of these cuts, the assured element of pension protection would be drastically curtailed.

Protection against Risk. Because the investment options and management of the individual accounts would be patterned after those of the federal employees' Thrift Savings Plan, investment risk on these accounts would be moderate and similar to that of the Individual Account plan. The minimum Social Security benefit in the Breaux-Gregg plan, which is equal to the poverty threshold for a worker with forty years of participation, would provide some protection to low earners if returns from their individual accounts turned out to be sub-par. This safety net, however, would become less meaningful over time because productivity growth will push up real incomes while the poverty threshold is adjusted only for inflation. The minimum benefit could undermine political support for the system if many low and moderate earners received pensions based on the guaranteed minimum rather than on the Social Security benefit formula. This development would weaken the fundamental relationship between earnings and contributions on the one hand and benefits on the other. The mandatory annuitization of a portion of the personal accounts would protect people from outliving their pensions.

Administrative Efficiency. The central administration and investment management of the personal accounts, investment in a restricted number of index funds, and mandatory annuitization would hold down overhead costs of the Breaux-Gregg plan. These costs, however, would exceed those of the Individual Account plan because of the complexity inherent in calculating the portion of each personal account that would have to be annuitized and the difficulties associated with administering both the annuity and the remaining balance.

National Saving. Because it does not raise payroll taxes, the Breaux-Gregg plan would add much less in the near term to national saving than the Individual Account plan. Unlike the accounts under the Personal Security Account plan, those of the Breaux-Gregg plan would not be considered good substitutes for IRAs or 401(k) plans.

Overall, we give the Twenty-first Century Retirement plan sponsored by Senators Breaux and Gregg a grade of C+ (see Table 7–6), see page 136.

TABLE 7–6
REPORT CARD FOR THE BREAUX-GREGG
(TWENTY-FIRST CENTURY RETIREMENT) PLAN

CRITERIA	GRADE
Adequacy, equity, and a fair return	C
Protection against risk	C
Administrative efficiency	C+
Increased national saving	B-
Overall grade	C+

RETAIN SOCIAL SECURITY WITH CHANGES TO RESTORE FINANCIAL BALANCE

The final approach to Social Security reform preserves the current system and continues to rely on a defined-benefit system to assure basic retirement income. Mandatory pensions would remain tied exclusively to each worker's past earnings and years of work, not to fluctuating asset prices.

BALL PLAN[9]

Robert M. Ball, a former commissioner of the Social Security Administration, has proposed to restore projected long-run financial balance by increasing payroll tax revenues, cutting benefits modestly, and investing part of the trust funds' reserves in equities (see the appendix to this chapter, page 147, and Table 7–1 for details). Investment of up to 40 percent of the reserves in common stocks by 2015 would close roughly half of the projected long-term deficit. Increased revenues, which would come from subjecting a greater pro-portion of benefits to the personal income tax and increasing the maximum earnings subject to the payroll tax, would contribute another one-third. Extending coverage to newly hired state and local workers and increasing from 35 to 38 the number of years of earnings used to compute benefits finish the job.

Benefit Adequacy and Equity. The Ball plan would provide larger benefits than any of the other plans described in this chapter, save the Feldstein plan, which would appropriate projected budget surpluses and then raise taxes or cut other program spending to boost benefits. Vulnerable groups would be well protected. The plan, however, does not modify the spouse's or survivor's benefits or attempt to modernize Social Security in other ways to reflect the economic and social changes that have occurred over the past half century.

Protection against Risk. Because this plan would rely exclusively on defined-benefit pensions, it would spare workers exposure to the risks to their basic pension income that are inherent in individual accounts.[10] Annual cost-of-living adjustments would preserve the purchasing power of benefits from inflation. However, the Ball plan would probably not permanently solve the Social Security fiscal imbalance. Because the plan proposes only modest changes, Social Security would eventually fall out of close long-run actuarial balance, even if all economic and demographic assumptions prove accurate. Unpleasant surprises could cause deficits to appear sooner. While further adjustments to benefits or taxes could close any shortfall, we think current public distrust of the retirement system and of government in general make it vital to adopt reforms that will restore financial balance and sustain it even if economic and demographic assumptions turn out to be overly optimistic.

Administrative Efficiency. The Ball plan would maintain the current low-cost administrative structure for taxes and benefits. It would incur small added costs associated with investing the trust funds' reserves in equities but should amount to no more than 1/100 of a percent of funds invested.[11]

National Saving. Because the Ball plan would cut benefits and raise taxes only modestly, it would contribute less to national saving than several of the other plans.

Overall, the Ball plan deserves a strong B+ (see Table 7–7, page 138).

TABLE 7–7
REPORT CARD FOR THE BALL PLAN

CRITERIA	GRADE
Adequacy, equity, and a fair return	A-
Protection against risk	B+
Administrative efficiency	A
Increased national saving	C+
Overall grade	B+

MAINTAIN STRUCTURE PLAN

The plan we described in Chapter 6 also relies exclusively on defined-benefit retirement pensions. The distinctive characteristic of this plan is the creation of a new Social Security Reserve Board (SSRB), modeled on the Federal Reserve Board, that would manage all financial operations of Social Security.[12] The operations of the Social Security system would be removed from the budget presentations of the executive and legislative branches. The SSRB would be charged with achieving, over the course of several decades, reserve balances similar in magnitude to those that would be required of private pension funds under the Employee Retirement Income Security Act. The trust funds' investments would be diversified among government bonds and private stocks and bonds. In addition, we propose somewhat larger benefit cuts than does the Ball plan to boost reserve accumulation and to raise national saving. The benefit cuts would be designed to reflect the changes that have occurred in the labor force and in life expectancy since the program was enacted.

Benefit Adequacy and Equity. This plan reduces benefits somewhat more than the Ball plan but it does not cut pensions significantly for vulnerable groups such as the disabled. Most surviving spouses would experience a small increase in benefits. Retired couples in which one spouse had little or no earnings history, on the other hand, would experience a modest decline in their pension. By investing the trust funds' reserves in a diversified portfolio, the plan would bring to people dependent on public pensions the higher yields that a broad portfolio of public and private bonds and stocks makes possible.

Protection against Risk. Like the Ball plan, the Maintain Structure plan preserves the key advantage of defined-benefit pension plans by spreading risks broadly among the general population. Benefits would remain fully protected from inflation. Because the plan more than closes the long-term deficit, uncertainty about future adjustment would be less than under the Ball plan. Furthermore, it incorporates a mechanism that would help to ensure that if the reformed program were to fall out of long-run actuarial balance in the future, policymakers would enact corrective measures.

Administrative Efficiency. This plan maintains all the administrative efficiencies of the current system.

National Saving. This plan would add moderately to national saving. It would isolate Social Security surpluses from the general budget process so that they are more likely than under current budget rules to add to national saving.

Nobody will be surprised if we award the plan we sketched out in Chapter 6 the top overall grade, an A- (see Table 7–8). That plan best meets the criteria we set forth earlier in this chapter.

TABLE 7–8
REPORT CARD FOR THE
MAINTAIN STRUCTURE PLAN

CRITERIA	GRADE
Adequacy, equity, and a fair return	B+
Protection against risk	A
Administrative efficiency	A
Increased national saving	B+
Overall grade	A-

CONCLUSION

No perfect way exists to reform the nation's mandatory retirement program; all plans involve tradeoffs among desirable objectives. Table 7–9 is our "grade sheet" for the seven plans. We did not give our plan a straight A because we think no plan that cuts benefits or raises taxes merits that grade. Furthermore, our plan—like all others—contains politically unpopular provisions that elected officials will find hard to endorse.

While investing Social Security's growing reserves, collectively or through individual accounts, in assets that have higher yields than government bonds can help, that policy change alone cannot close the projected deficit. To finish the job, future retirees will have to accept smaller benefits than those promised under current law or future workers will have to pay higher taxes. The weightlifter's maxim, "no pain, no gain," applies also to pension policy. The question is: Whose gain and whose pain?

TABLE 7–9
SUMMARY REPORT CARD

PLAN	GRADE
Personal Security Account	C
Feldstein	C
Individual Account	B
Moynihan	D
Breaux-Gregg	C+
Ball	B+
Maintain Structure	A-

Appendix to Chapter 7

FEATURES OF THE PERSONAL
SECURITY ACCOUNT (PSA) PLAN [a]

GENERAL CHANGES

◆ All newly hired state and local workers would be brought into the system.

◆ The retirement earnings test would be repealed.

◆ The scheduled increase to 67 in the age at which unreduced benefits are paid would be accelerated to 2011 and raised thereafter to reflect improved adult life expectancy.

◆ The age of initial benefit eligibility would be raised gradually from 62 to 64 by 2011.

◆ Disability benefits would be reduced gradually, for workers who are currently young, by up to 30 percent.

◆ Payroll taxes would be increased 1.52 percentage points for the next seventy-two years.

FOR WORKERS UNDER AGE 25

FIRST TIER

◆ Workers with thirty-five or more years of covered employment would receive a flat, inflation-protected benefit equal to 76 percent of the benefit paid to low-wage workers under the current system. This benefit would be reduced 2 percent for each year of work under thirty-five years and by up to 30 percent if claimed earlier than the standard retirement age.

◆ Spouses with fewer than ten years of work would receive a flat benefit equal to half the benefit payable to the primary worker; widows and widowers would receive at least three-quarters of a couple's combined benefit.

◆ The flat benefit and spouse's, survivors, and disibility benefits would be financed by employers' payroll tax (6.2 percent of covered earnings) and 1.2 percentage points of the employees' payroll tax.

◆ All of the flat benefit would be subject to income tax.

SECOND TIER

◆ Personal Security Accounts would be established through a financial institution of the worker's choice. Five percentage points of the worker's earnings would be deposited in these accounts.

◆ Individuals could invest balances under rules similar to those governing Individual Retirement Accounts.

◆ At the age of initial eligibility for first tier benefits, each person could use the accumulated balance to buy an annuity, withdraw funds on a fixed schedule, or hold funds for transfer to heirs through bequest; all withdrawals would be exempt from income tax.

Continued on the following page

FEATURES OF THE PERSONAL
SECURITY ACCOUNT (PSA) PLAN[1] (CONT'D)

FOR WORKERS AGE 25 TO 55

FIRST TIER

◆ These workers would receive pensions from a blended system based mostly on Social Security for older workers and mostly on the First Tier of the new system for younger workers.

SECOND TIER

◆ These workers would have the same Personal Security Accounts as for younger workers, but smaller amounts would accumulate because deposits would have been made for a briefer period.

FOR RETIREES AND WORKERS OVER AGE 55

◆ These workers would receive Social Security, with general modifications listed above.

---

a. *Report of the 1994–1996 Advisory Council on Social Security,* Volume I: Findings and Recommendations (Washington, D.C.: U.S. Government Printing Office, 1997).

FEATURES OF THE INDIVIDUAL ACCOUNTS (IA) PLAN [a]

CHANGES IN SOCIAL SECURITY

♦ Benefits would be reduced gradually for all newly retired workers with average adjusted lifetime earnings above about $5,724 (in 1998, and adjusted upward by the growth in average wages).

♦ The number of years of earnings used to compute benefits would be increased from thirty-five to thirty-eight.

♦ Social Security benefits would be taxed the same as contributory private pensions.

♦ All newly hired state and local workers would be brought into the system.

♦ The scheduled increase to 67 in the age at which unreduced benefits are paid would be accelerated to 2011 and raised thereafter to reflect improved adult life expectancy.

♦ The spouse's benefit would be cut from one-half to one-third of the primary worker's benefit, but surviving spouses would be assured a benefit equal to at least three-quarters of the couple's combined benefits.

PERSONAL ACCOUNTS

♦ A new 1.6 percentage point payroll tax would be imposed on employees and its proceeds would be deposited in individual accounts that resembled the accounts held in the federal employees' Thrift Savings Plan (see Box 6–4).

♦ When workers retired, their account balances would have to be converted into inflation-protected annuities.

a. *Report of the 1994–1996 Advisory Council on Social Security,* Volume I: Findings and Recommendations (Washington, D.C.: U.S. Government Printing Office, 1997).

FEATURES OF THE MOYNIHAN
(SOCIAL SECURITY SOLVENCY) PLAN[a]

BENEFIT CUTS

◆ The annual cost-of-living adjustment to benefits would be 1 percentage point less than the change in the Consumer Price Index.

◆ The age at which unreduced benefits are paid would be increased two months each year until it reached 68 in 2017, and by one month every two years thereafter until it reached 70 in 2065.

◆ The number of years of earnings used to calculate benefits would be increased gradually from thirty-five to thirty-eight.

REVENUE INCREASES

◆ Benefits would be taxed in the same fashion as contributory private pensions.

◆ The maximum taxable earnings would be increased gradually by about 18 percent.

OTHER CHANGES

◆ The payroll tax rate would be cut by 2 percentage points and then raised gradually to support the system on a pay-as-you-go basis.

◆ Voluntary retirement savings accounts would be established for those workers who wanted to contribute 1 percent of earnings to them. Employers would have to match the employees' contributions. The worker could choose to have the account managed by the government's Voluntary Investment Fund Board, which would offer investments similar to those available to federal employees in the Thrift Savings Plan or by a private financial institution. Account balances could be withdrawn in any form upon retirement.

◆ All newly hired state and local workers would be brought into the system.

◆ The retirement earnings test would be repealed.

a. S.1792, 105th Congress, 2d Session, and "Senator Daniel Patrick Moynihan Social Security Solvency Act of 1998, Brief Description of Provisions and Supplementary Materials from the Congressional Budget Office and the Social Security Administration," mimeo, March 1998.

FEATURES OF THE BREAUX-GREGG
(TWENTY-FIRST CENTURY RETIREMENT) PLAN[a]

CHANGES IN SOCIAL SECURITY

◆ The spouse's benefit would be gradually reduced from one-half to one-third of the primary worker's benefit.

◆ Benefits would be computed by summing all of a worker's adjusted earnings and dividing by forty.

◆ Benefits would be reduced gradually for all newly retired workers with average adjusted lifetime earnings above about $5,724 (in 1998 and adjusted upward by the growth in average wages).

◆ All newly hired state and local workers would be covered.

◆ The age at which unreduced benefits are paid would be increased two months a year, reaching age 70 in 2029, and by one month every year and a half thereafter, reaching 72 in 2065.

◆ The age of initial eligibility for benefits would be increased two months a year, reaching age 65 in 2029, and by one month every year and a half thereafter, reaching 67 in 2065.

◆ The retirement earnings test would be eliminated for all those above the age at which unreduced benefits are available.

◆ The early retirement penalty and the delayed retirement credit would be increased to make them more accurate.

◆ The annual cost-of-living adjustment would be reduced to account for a portion of the bias remaining in the measured CPI.

NEW MINIMUM BENEFIT

◆ A minimum benefit would be established equal to 60 percent of the poverty threshold for those with twenty years of covered earnings and rising by 2 percentage points per additional year to 100 percent of the poverty threshold for those with forty or more years of covered earnings.

PERSONAL ACCOUNTS

◆ Personal accounts similar in investment options and management to accounts held in the federal employees' Thrift Savings Plan (see Box 6-4) would be established using 2 percentage points of the existing payroll tax. Supplemental voluntary contributions of up to $2,000 per year would be permitted.

◆ Upon retirement, a portion of the accounts' balances would have to be used to purchase an inflation-protected annuity that, when added to the scaled back Social Security benefit, met a minimum threshold for retirement income adequacy. Excess balances could be withdrawn according to the retiree's needs.

---

a. S. 2313, 105th Congress, 2d Session, and National Commission on Retirement Policy, "The 21st Century Retirement Security Plan," Center for Strategic and International Studies, May 19, 1998.

FEATURES OF THE BALL
(RESTORE LONG-TERM BALANCE) PLAN[a]

BENEFIT CUTS

♦ The number of years of earnings used to compute benefits would be increased from thirty-five to thirty-eight.

REVENUE INCREASES

♦ Benefits would be taxed in the same fashion as contributory private pensions.

♦ The maximum earnings subject to the payroll tax would be increased gradually by about 18 percent.

OTHER CHANGES

♦ All newly hired state and local workers would be brought into the system.

♦ By 2015, 40 percent of the trust funds' reserves would be invested in a diversified portfolio of common stocks.

---

a. Robert M. Ball with Thomas N. Bethell, *Straight Talk About Social Security: An Analysis of the Issues in the Current Debate*, Century Foundation/Twentieth Century Fund Report (New York: Century Foundation Press, 1998).

8

THE POLITICS OF REFORM

If references to Social Security as the third rail of American politics were once valid, someone has turned off the electricity. Politicians who once said, "Touch it and you die" now seem eager to propose far-reaching changes to the system.

In fact, Social Security was never untouchable. Congress significantly curtailed Social Security benefits twice over the past twenty-five years—in 1977 and 1983. None of the elected officials who supported these cuts suffered political electrocution. Most people, then as now, accepted benefit cuts and tax increases that were necessary to restore the program's financial balance.

The one occasion when elected officials received a high-voltage jolt was in 1982, when President Reagan proposed large cuts in retirement, survivor's, and disability benefits that would have taken effect just a few months after enactment. No member of the Senate could be found to sponsor the president's plan. This experience, arising from an ill-considered proposal, gave rise to the vivid but inaccurate "third-rail" metaphor. The vital political lesson suggested by the complete record, however, is that Congresses and presidents can address the program's problems without fear of political retribution if the public understands that action is necessary to maintain a stable, fair, and adequate retirement system. Even then, it helps if a sizable contingent from both political parties engages in the effort so that neither party later can clobber the other for "betraying the elderly."

Whether conditions are now ripe for action is unclear. Social Security is far from collapse. The program's receipts now exceed expenditures by more than $100 billion a year, and surpluses will persist for two decades. But public understanding is growing that the retirement of the baby boomers will raise costs, that the program's projected long-term deficit must eventually be closed, and that prompt action can forestall a later crisis. President Clinton's call during the 1998 State of the Union Address for a national discussion on how best to strengthen the program for the long run received bipartisan commendation. Furthermore, senators and representatives have introduced bills that address Social Security's long-run problem in various ways, including through substantial benefit reductions, tax increases, and radical structural reforms. None has been punished at the voting booth.

The emergence of favorable economic conditions—budget surpluses, low unemployment, and low inflation—has also improved the environment for reform. When the budget is in deficit those pushing for benefit cuts or payroll tax increases to strengthen Social Security are vulnerable to the charge that they are trying to balance the overall budget, pay for income tax cuts, or finance a favorite expenditure program by restraining Social Security. In fact, the tables have turned—several recent reform proposals call for devoting a portion of the unified budget surplus to shoring up Social Security (see Box 8–1).

Although divided government—Republican majorities in Congress and Democratic control of the White House—makes some legislation more difficult to pass, it may actually improve the prospects for reform of Social Security. Closing a projected Social Security deficit is always difficult, but sharing responsibility for policy changes may make it a bit easier because elected officials never want to hand opponents issues that can be used against them.

Even in this relatively benign environment, Republicans and Democrats will find it hard to agree on whether to modify the structure of Social Security and how to close the projected long-run deficit. Philosophical differences will obstruct agreement, as they have since Social Security's inception. Crass considerations of political advantage will have to be overcome. Current surpluses will make procrastination tempting, for any comprehensive reform will require some sacrifice. Those whose interests are adversely affected will try to shift burdens to others. They will argue that current and projected surpluses make more study and analysis desirable and hasty action unnecessary.

BOX 8-1
WHAT DOES IT MEAN TO DEVOTE THE UNIFIED
BUDGET SURPLUS TO SOCIAL SECURITY?

In fiscal year 1998, the Social Security program is projected to run a surplus of $99 billion while the budget for all other government operations are expected to run a deficit of $28 billion. The unified budget—the sum of Social Security's bottom line and that for the government's other programs—is projected to register a $71 billion surplus, the first in twenty-nine years.

Some lawmakers have introduced legislation that would transfer all, or a portion, of future unified budget surpluses to Social Security.[a] But what does this mean at a time when the only surplus the government is experiencing is that registered by Social Security? Wouldn't such proposals just be giving back to Social Security what it already has?

Suppose Congress transferred all or part of the $71 billion unified budget surplus projected for 1998 to the trust funds. The Social Security trustees would be required by law to invest these resources, like other reserves, in securities issued by the Treasury. But the resources transferred to the trust funds could not, in the first instance, be used by Social Security to buy back government bonds held by the public. Instead, the Treasury would have to issue new securities to the trust funds. Not needing the resources it receives from Social Security to fund government programs, the Treasury would use these proceeds from securities issued to Social Security to repurchase government debt held by the public. In the end, the act of transferring the surplus from the Treasury Department to Social Security has no effect on the amount of debt held by the general public.

Because the transfer of the unified budget surplus would increase the trust funds' balances, the date at which the Social Security program would become insolvent would be postponed. However, this would not affect the adjustments—the tax increases, reductions in other programs, or increased borrowing from the public—that would be required when, after 2020, the trust funds will have to begin to redeem their government securities to meet benefits obligations that exceeded program receipts. Moreover, transferring the unified budget surplus to Social Security would not, under current budget accounting rules, change the unified budget surplus, which, after all, is the surplus in the Social Security program plus the balance in the government's other accounts.

If the unified budget surplus were transferred to Social Security with instructions that these resources be used to purchase private assets, the amount of Treasury debt held by the public would not fall. Commensurately, debt service payments would not decline as one expects when the unified budget is in surplus. Purchases of private assets by the trust funds or by individual accounts would be considered an expenditure, one that would transform the unified budget from surplus to balance.[b] These investments would generate a flow of interest and dividend payments that would be similar to the reduced debt service in the previous example.

---

a. For example, during the 105th Congress, Charles Rangel, ranking Democrat on the Ways and Means Committee, introduced H.R. 3207, which required that Treasury establish a Save Social Security First Reserve Fund into which the unified budget surplus would be transferred at the end of each fiscal year until legislation was adopted to reform Social Security. John Kasich, chairman of the House Budget Committee, introduced legislation (H.R. 3456) that would have used a portion of the unified budget surplus to establish personal accounts.

b. Purchase of bonds may be evaluated under credit reform score keeping, which would register the transaction as having little effect on spending.

As Americans weigh the merits of alternative reforms, they should not lose sight of two political questions about every plan:

◆   Can it be enacted now?

◆   Can it be sustained?

POLITICAL SUPPORT FOR ENACTMENT

However high a plan may rank on our criteria for reform, it is no more than intellectual wheel spinning if it cannot generate the political support needed to pass Congress and secure the president's signature well before the retirement of the baby boomers is in full swing. In particular, a politically viable plan requires at least grudging acceptance from most of the parties that have an important stake in Social Security reform, including:

◆   workers, whose interests will vary depending on age, earnings, family circumstances, and whether they participate in a private pension plan;

◆   unions;

◆   employers, whose views may depend on the size, wage level, and stability of their workforce; whether they offer a pension plan, and, if they do, the extent to which that plan is integrated with Social Security; and the degree to which their payroll and benefit systems are automated;

◆   governors, congressional representatives, state legislators, and civil servants from states that have elected to remain outside the Social Security system; and,

◆   the retired and organizations that represent them;

◆   a wide range of business and civic groups concerned about the nation's mandatory retirement system.

None of these groups has an absolute veto, but loud vigorous opposition from any will cause some members of Congress to oppose a particular proposal and make other members cautious about endorsing major changes in Social Security.

CLOSING A DEFICIT IS NEVER POPULAR

The effort to close the overall federal deficit that has occupied Congress and successive presidents since 1983 has made two facts clear: raising taxes or cutting spending is never easy and rarely popular, and there is nothing like good luck, in the form of unexpectedly robust economic growth and larger-than-anticipated tax collections, to make the job easier. Let's start with "luck."

COULD THE PROJECTIONS BE WRONG?

The projections of the Social Security actuaries are regularly attacked as overly optimistic by advocates of radical change and as overly pessimistic by advocates of the status quo. Both are probably right in detail but wrong in their overall evaluations. The projections are based on assumptions that all fall within the range of views held by responsible private experts who make their livelihoods forecasting long-run demographic, labor market, and economic conditions. The political debate should, therefore, accept the projections as plausible indications of the future. Congress should not count on a political free lunch to spare them the need to cut benefits or raise taxes.

TAX INCREASES

Although U.S. taxes are low by international standards, the anti-tax mood is so strong that Congress is not likely to close the projected long-term Social Security deficit primarily by raising taxes. The more interesting question is whether small tax increases that prevent the need for deep benefit cuts will be acceptable as part of a broad program to reform Social Security. Some plans try to overcome opposition to higher taxes by earmarking the added revenues for personal accounts and by exempting employers from paying the new tax.

COST-OF-LIVING ADJUSTMENTS

Proposals to reduce annual cost-of-living adjustments will—and we think should—provoke powerful opposition. Analysts agree that the Consumer Price Index (CPI) overstates inflation. But they continue to argue over how large the overstatement is and how, practically, the overstatement can be eliminated. We see no justification for failing to compensate pensioners fully for properly measured inflation. Spokespersons for the elderly and disabled will protest loudly and effectively that denial of full inflation adjustments cumulates over time and would create real hardship.

Taxpayers would also oppose less than full cost-of-living adjustments. Each year, inflation adjustments increase the personal exemptions, the standard deduction, and the amount of income subject to the lowest tax rates. If full cost-of-living adjustments are denied to Social Security beneficiaries, it would be hard to sustain other cost-of-living adjustments, including those in other indexed benefits, including those paid to veterans, retired civil servants, recipients of student loans, and others who participate in programs that are adjusted annually by the CPI. This connection between cost-of-living adjustments in Social Security and similar adjustments in other programs makes any denial of full adjustment unlikely.

HOW MANY VOTES DO THEY HAVE?

Joseph Stalin cynically derided the importance of the papacy during World War II by asking, "How many divisions does the Pope have?" A contemporary cynic might ask us and other policy analysts how many votes we have for the various analytically sound, but politically unappealing, reforms that we recommend. The cases for extending Social Security to all new state and local workers, for taxing Social Security benefits like private pensions, and for increasing the age at which unreduced benefits are paid are all strong. But opinion polls reveal very little support for these policies. Extending coverage would provide state and local employees with better disability, survivor, and spouse's benefits, and improved pension protection against inflation. But many representatives from currently uncovered states—which happen to include political heavyweights such as California, Texas, Massachusetts, and Ohio—will oppose extending coverage. They understand that the average earnings of their employees exceed average Social Security earnings. By maintaining separate retirement systems, these states can avoid some of the costs of the assistance Social Security provides to low earners. Affected jurisdictions will argue that integrating their pension plans for new hires with Social Security is an impossibly complex task. The fact that the federal government brought all its new employees into Social Security starting in 1984 indicates that this argument is substantively weak, but may not impair its political usefulness.

Extending to Social Security benefits the same personal income tax rules that apply to other contributory pensions also makes sense. Once again, however, the opposition to such a tax change is likely to be strong, especially among middle- and upper-middle-income retirees. High-income retirees have little at stake, because legislation enacted in 1983 and 1993 already subject their benefits to tax. Personal exemptions and the standard deduction will continue to shield benefits of low-income retirees from tax. Middle-income beneficiaries, however, will face higher taxes. Retirees who count on this income are not likely to be mollified by the fact that most of the benefits they receive represent returns far in excess of the payroll taxes they paid as individuals and that such returns are routinely taxed when they come through contributory private pensions.

Finally, benefit cuts in some form will be needed if taxes are not raised significantly. Polls indicate that the public thinks current benefits are, if anything, too low and does not want to see them cut. Elected officials read polls—and their mail. No matter what form a benefit cut takes, it runs afoul of the political Hippocratic oath—"at least do no *obvious* harm"—and supporting votes will be hard to come by.

A KEY PRINCIPLE—MAKE HASTE SLOWLY

These and other potential flashpoints of opposition may be defused by lengthy phase-in periods. President Reagan ran into a firestorm in 1982 when he proposed benefit cuts that would have taken effect only a few months after enactment. Yet Congress subsequently found far larger changes acceptable, in part because they were phased in gradually. Specifically, Congress cut benefits roughly 13 percent by raising the age at which unreduced benefits are paid from 65 to 67, but delayed the start of the cuts until the year 2000 and spread them over twenty-two years. Similarly, while payroll tax rates have been raised from 9.2 to 12.4 percent of covered earnings since 1971, and additional increases have been made in the portion of earnings subject to tax, the increases came in nine small hikes, none larger than 0.72 percentage points and four of 0.2 percentage points or less.

SUSTAINING POLITICAL SUPPORT

Social Security is too large and important to the economy and too central to the lives of millions of individuals to undergo frequent change. If participants are to make rational lifetime personal saving plans, they need to know that the core structure of the nation's basic retirement program will remain stable. Employers whose private pension plans supplement the mandatory public system want a public pension system that is not in constant flux. Political sustainability is a vital attribute of any reform plan. A plan that contains the political seeds of its own demise or transformation is therefore a bad plan.

The current system has passed the test of political sustainability *summa cum laude*. It has generated powerful—some would say, excessive—support for its preservation. Workers who have paid taxes for years come to feel that they have an earned right to receive pensions when they become old or disabled. While advocates of change may wish the current system elicited a bit less support, no program that fails to develop and maintain loyal political allegiance can long survive in a democracy.

Proposals to base a retirement pension system on private accounts are likely to fail the durability test for several reasons. First, keeping funds locked up until workers retire will be hard. The history of Individual Retirement Accounts (IRAs) is illustrative. Over time, pressures have mounted to permit individuals to gain access to IRA balances before retirement. Congress has succumbed to those pressures, giving individuals access to these accounts under a lengthening list of conditions. Similar pressures are likely to arise with respect to any individual accounts. Workers could increasingly come to view these accounts as similar to other private saving vehicles. The first step would be permission to use the accounts to pay for medical emergencies, then to pay for first-time home purchases, education, or living expenses during extended unemployment. Each new and worthy use would further undermine the primary goal of assuring adequate retirement income.

The inevitable ups and downs of financial markets are also likely to jeopardize the stability of a system based on personal accounts. Figure 3-1 showed that the value of pensions that individual accounts could support would have fallen more than 60 percent between 1969 and 1976 if reserves were invested in common stocks. Similar, if somewhat smaller, risks threaten funds invested in long-term bonds. Congress would face overwhelming pressures to intervene to protect investments or to provide supplements for cohorts whose replacement rates were smaller than those of earlier cohorts. Such bailouts would transform individual accounts into something quite different from what advocates are proposing now. Whether or not such hybrids would be desirable, the full ramifications of individual accounts should be considered before any action is taken to create them.

Plans that combine traditional Social Security with new private accounts contain an element of political risk. The personal accounts component of such hybrid systems would pay a return equal to the yield of whatever assets depositors chose for their portfolios. The traditional Social Security component would provide workers with smaller benefits per dollar of payroll taxes than the personal accounts because most of the taxes would be used to support benefits for previous retirees. In addition, some of the taxes paid by high earners would go to support the social functions of Social Security—the extra benefits for low earners and families with children. None of the taxes deposited into personal accounts would be siphoned off for these purposes. Because Social Security would continue to bear responsibility for supporting past retirees and providing social assistance, it would appear to generate lower returns, especially for middle and high earners, even if the trust funds earned returns as high as or higher than those of individual accounts. After comparing the returns on personal accounts with the apparent yield offered by Social Security, many workers would conclude that they could do better if they were permitted to shift payroll taxes from Social Security to their individual accounts. The conclusion would be false, as we showed in Chapter 5, because workers would have to keep supporting benefits for current retirees. But the threat to the political viability of Social Security would be real. It is doubtful whether such a system would be politically sustainable.

The problem would be particularly acute in hybrid plans that provide workers both a flat benefit and personal accounts. High earners would quickly realize that they could earn much higher returns if they were permitted to shift the payroll taxes they paid to support the flat benefit to their personal accounts. The political coalition on behalf of the flat benefit would weaken, creating incentives for Congress to let the flat benefit languish, especially during periods of budget deficits when foregoing annual increases in the flat benefit could be an acceptable way to cut federal spending. A central question about such plans, therefore, is whether they would protect low earners *in practice* as well as they appear to do *on paper*. Those who support Social Security in part because it has created a stable and mutually supportive coalition on behalf of pensions for everyone and social assistance for low earners have reason to be concerned that various individual account proposals would put social assistance in jeopardy.

CONCLUSION

America has a rare opportunity to restore financial balance to the nation's mandatory retirement system and modernize it for the twenty-first century. The economy is strong. Inflation is well controlled. The federal budget is in surplus for the first time in three decades. Demographic pressures are low; the proportion of the population that is elderly will rise little between 1998 and 2008—from 14.9 percent to 15.7 percent.

These favorable circumstances will not last. The leading edge of the baby-boom generation will reach retirement age in 2008. In 2019, more than twice as many people will turn 62 as did in 1998. As the baby boomers retire, spending on Social Security, Medicare, Supplemental Security Income, and Medicaid will rise rapidly. Current projections indicate that today's budget surpluses will be replaced by growing deficits unless future obligations are curtailed or taxes are increased.

Both current and future conditions make prompt action to reform Social Security highly desirable. As more baby boomers retire, the politics of reform will become increasingly difficult and the options more circumscribed. Since benefit cuts usually must be imposed very gradually, payroll tax increases will become the only realistic method of closing emerging deficits. Early action to close the projected long-term deficits of Social Security permits other changes that can be phased in gradually. Delay will be politically tempting—why enact benefits or raise taxes when current revenues continue to exceed expenditures? Delay would be a grave mistake, however, as it will make future actions more difficult and certainly more wrenching.

Appendix

Thumbnail Descriptions of Other Major Social Security Reform Plans

Many more proposals to reform or replace Social Security have been put forward than the seven plans evaluated in Chapter 7. This appendix provides brief summaries of several of them. This list is by no means exhaustive, but it provides some sense of the types of proposals that have been advanced.

Committee for Economic Development (CED)[1]

The CED plan would create individual accounts roughly twice as large as those in the Individual Accounts plan described in Chapter 7, but the two plans are otherwise similar. Like the Individual Accounts plan, the CED proposal would cut retirement, survivor's, and disability benefits enough to hold the payroll tax rate at 12.4 percent. The CED plan would reduce benefits by changing the benefit formula to reduce the replacement rates for all but low earners and by increasing from thirty-five to forty the number of years of earnings that are averaged when calculating benefits. In addition, benefits would be cut by raising by two months a year starting in 2000 the age at which unreduced benefits are paid. After 2030, when the age for receiving unreduced benefits reaches 70, the age for receiving full benefits would be linked to increases in life expectancy in a way that would keep the ratio of years in retirement to working years constant. The CED plan would gradually reduce the spouse's benefit from one-half to one-third of the primary earner's benefit and eliminate the earnings test on beneficiaries.

Social Security benefits would be taxed like contributory private pensions under this plan and all newly hired state and local employees would be covered. An increase in the payroll tax of 3 percentage points would fund individual accounts modeled on existing 401(k) accounts. Individuals could invest these funds in any approved asset. Upon reaching retirement age, beneficiaries could convert balances into annuities or withdraw funds gradually. Any balance remaining at death would be part of the decedent's estate.

The accounts created under the CED plan would resemble Individual Retirement Accounts; accordingly, administrative costs would be higher than under the Individual Accounts plan, which is modeled on the Thrift Savings Plan. As with the Individual Accounts plan, disability and retirement benefits would be cut to inadequate levels for some pensioners.

THE PORTER PLAN[2]

The plan crafted by Representative John Porter (Republican of Illinois) would give workers an irrevocable choice between remaining under Social Security or diverting 10 percentage points of the payroll tax to personal retirement accounts. For those opting for the personal accounts, the remaining 2.4 percentage points of payroll tax would flow for ten years to the Social Security Trust Funds and then cease. Workers over age 30 would be awarded government bonds that reflected their past Social Security contributions; workers under age 30 would receive no such bonds. These "recognition bonds" would be redeemed for monthly benefits upon retirement. Workers who established individual accounts could deposit additional nondeductible contributions of up to 20 percent of earnings.

Personal retirement account balances could be invested with any federally approved investment company under rules similar to those that now apply to IRAs. A portion of these accounts would have to be used to purchase adequate disability insurance and survivor insurance. The federal government would guarantee a minimum retirement benefit equal to the lesser of 40 percent of average preretirement income of 95 percent of expected Social Security benefits. After age 59 1/2 workers could choose to convert their accumulations into an annuity or withdraw funds gradually. Distributions would be subject to the same income tax rules that apply to Social Security benefits. There would be no spouse's benefits for those choosing personal accounts unless the retiree purchased a joint annuity. Funds remaining at workers' deaths would be included in their estates. Workers who stay in Social Security would be eligible for reduced benefits, which would be lowered by raising the age at which unreduced benefits are paid to 70 by 2029 and by shifting from wage indexing to price indexing of the benefit formula.

The practice under Social Security of providing larger benefits relative to earnings for low earners than for high earners would be abandoned for those choosing the individual accounts option. The only exception is that the minimum federally guaranteed benefit would be more likely to exceed accumulations for low earners than for high earners. In addition, the guarantee would boost the benefits of those with personal accounts who worked intermittently or experienced poor returns on investments. All of these workers would have an incentive to choose highly risky investments because they would stand to lose nothing if the investment failed but would retain any gains. The reductions in Social Security benefits would make that option progressively less attractive. After thirty years, benefits would be approximately 45 percent lower than promised under current law, but taxes would be unchanged.

The Porter plan would be costly and difficult to administer. Employers would be hard pressed to remit contributions to personal accounts within ten business days of when workers receive their paychecks as the proposal requires. Fees and charges imposed by the account managers would be as high as those in the Personal Security Accounts plan described in Chapter 7. The Social Security administration would have to collect earning information on workers with established individual accounts to determine whether they were affected by the minimum annuity guarantee. Calculating and administering the recognition bonds would be difficult.

THE SANFORD PLAN[3]

Representative Mark Sanford (Republican of South Carolina) proposes to replace Social Security with a system of individual accounts financed by payroll taxes of 4 percent each on workers and employers (8 percent on the self-employed). Workers could deposit unlimited additional amounts in their accounts. The new system would be mandatory for workers entering the labor force in the year 2000 and later, but optional for older workers, who would have to make an irrevocable decision on whether to remain in Social Security or switch to the new system. All earnings on individual accounts would be tax exempt until paid out as benefits. Funds in a worker's account would have to be invested in low to moderate risk index funds until the balance was sufficient to support an annual annuity equivalent to $8,500 in year 1996 dollars—the earnings of a full time worker at the minimum wage. Balances above those needed to meet this minimum could be invested in any assets. No withdrawals would be permitted until age 62. After that age, withdrawals could be made as long as the account contained sufficient funds to purchase the minimum annuity. The federal government would insure accounts up to the minimum annuity level with financing from general revenues. The plan would extend coverage to all newly hired state and local employees.

Workers who remained in Social Security would face reduced replacement rates from changes in the benefit formula. The age of unreduced benefits would be gradually increased to 70 by 2029. The cost-of-living adjustment would be reduced by 0.5 percentage points and limited in amount to that paid to the thirtieth percentile benefit. Payroll taxes of an additional 2.9 percent each on workers and employers would be retained to finance residual benefits under the Social Security system. These revenues would flow directly to the Treasury and the trust funds would be abolished. There would be no spouse's benefits under the personal retirement accounts. For those still covered by Social Security, the spouse's benefit would gradually be reduced from one-half to one-third of the primary worker's benefit.

The Sanford plan is incomplete, as it would create a large budget deficit—payroll taxes would be sharply reduced for workers who do not remain under Social Security, but Social Security benefits would not be materially cut at first. A "bipartisan" commission would be created to deal with this massive issue. The Sanford plan would end the payment of larger benefits relative to earnings for low earners than for high earners, except for the minimum-wage guarantee that would affect very low earners. The plan would be expensive to administer.

THE SMITH PLAN[4]

Representative Nick Smith's (Republican of Michigan) plan would establish mandatory individual accounts, which would eventually replace Social Security. Payroll taxes would remain at 6.2 percent each for employees and employers, but 2.5 percent of payroll would be deposited in individual accounts with investment companies regulated by the Treasury Department. The proportion of taxes allocated to individual accounts would gradually rise leaving reserves under the residual Social Security system of 50 percent of the next year's outlays. Workers could make supplementary voluntary contributions of up to $2,000 annually that would be partially deductible. In addition, one-third of the previous year's budget surplus would be divided equally among all individual accounts. If the personal account of a retirement age worker could not support a benefit at least as large as Social Security benefits under the current system, the Treasury would make up the difference.

Social Security benefits would be cut sharply—by raising to 69 by 2015 the age at which unreduced benefits are paid, by raising the early entitlement age to 65 by 2011, by extending the benefit computation period to 39 years, by lowering the replacement factors in the benefit formula, and by cutting the spouse's benefit from 50 percent to 33 1/3 percent. In addition, the plan would extend coverage to all newly hired state and local employees. It would income-test the benefits of current retirees once their pension payouts have equaled their payroll tax contributions plus estimated interest earnings on these funds.

This plan curtails benefits rapidly and allocates uncertain amounts to personal retirement accounts. For an extended transition period, retirees would lose far more in reduced Social Security than they would gain from accumulations in personal retirement accounts. It is estimated that the plan would run deficits of up to $85 billion annually for about fifteen years.

PERSONAL SECURITY SYSTEM[5]

The Personal Security System plan, developed by economists Laurence Kotlikoff and Jeffrey Sachs, would rely exclusively on personal retirement accounts. Of the current 12.4 percent payroll tax, 3.7 percentage points would be used to support disability and survivor benefits under current law. The remaining 8.7 percentage points would be redirected into personal accounts invested in a single international index portfolio of stocks, bonds, and real estate. The managers of this fund would be required to minimize administrative costs and avoid excessive risk. Half of a couple's combined contributions would be credited to each spouse's personal retirement account. Supplemental contributions, financed from general revenues, would boost accumulations and subsequent retirement incomes of low earners, but the exact structure of the supplements has not been specified. Accumulated balances would be converted into an inflation-indexed annuity over a ten-year period as workers approached retirement age.

Current retirees would remain under Social Security. All workers over 21 would receive all Social Security benefits accrued before the new law took effect.[6] Since Social Security benefits would be unreduced for retirees and those nearing retirement but payroll taxes would no longer be used to finance continuing Social Security retirement benefits, the Personal Security System plan needs an alternative revenue source. A national value-added or business cash-flow tax, with initial rates between 8 and 10 percent, would supply the necessary revenue; rates would decline gradually to about 2 percent after forty years.

THE KERREY/SIMPSON PLAN[7]

The proposal made by Senator Robert Kerrey (Democrat of Nebraska) and former senator Alan Simpson (Republican of Wyoming) would create individual accounts about 25 percent larger than those of the

Individual Accounts plan. Unlike the Individual Accounts plan, it would not raise payroll taxes. Accordingly, benefit cuts under the Kerrey/Simpson plan are larger than under the Individual Accounts plan. Deposits in individual accounts would equal 2 percent of covered earnings for people under age 55 when the plan begins. The funds could be invested either with a new government Personal Investment Fund managed like the Thrift Savings Plan for federal employees or in an Individual Retirement Account.

The Kerrey/Simpson plan would not adjust benefits for the first 0.5 percentage points of inflation and would cap adjustments at the amount given to workers at the thirtieth percentile of benefits. In addition, the Kerrey/Simpson plan would cut benefits by raising the age at which unreduced benefits are paid to age 70 by 2029 and by one month every two years thereafter, by modifying the benefit formula to reduce all but the lowest benefits, and by reducing the spouse's benefit from one-third to one-half of the primary worker's benefit. Other changes include extending coverage to all state and local workers, investing a portion of Social Security reserves in common stocks, and shifting to the Social Security trust funds' revenues from the taxation of Social Security benefits that are now deposited in the Medicare trust fund.

THE INVESTMENT-BASED SOCIAL SECURITY APPROACH[8]

Senator Phil Gramm (Republican of Texas) has issued a "feasibility study" for a plan that would give workers the option of remaining in Social Security or establishing an individual account. Workers would continue to pay 12.4 percent of covered earnings in payroll taxes. Those who established individual accounts would be credited with balances of 3 percent of earnings each year. These balances would be invested in approved investment organizations subject to regulation by a newly created private/public board. Until the new plan is fully in effect, workers would receive retirement benefits equal to those currently payable under Social Security plus 20 percent of the annuity that accumulations in their personal accounts would support. Eventually, workers would receive a benefit equal to 120 percent of current Social Security benefits. To pay for the extra costs of supporting both current Social Security benefits and deposits in individual accounts, the Gramm prospectus would rely on revenue from three sources: projected surpluses in the unified budget, redemption of 29 percent of accumulated Social Security reserves, and assumed increases in corporate tax revenues corresponding to earnings on assets held in individual accounts.

NOTES

1

1. Employee Benefit Research Institute, *The 1997 Retirement Confidence Survey: Summary of Findings*, Employee Benefit Research Institute, Washington, D.C., 1998. Fully half of respondents age 33 or younger say they want to retire before their fifty-sixth birthday.

2. Daniel Yankelovich, *Coming to Public Judgment: Making Democracy Work in a Complex World*, Frank W. Abrams Lectures (Syracuse, N.Y.: Syracuse University Press, 1991).

3. These estimates assume that the earnings of the 30-year-old rise 3 percent more than inflation each year, the return on saving is 5 percent more than inflation, and the individual dies at age 85. For information on retirement saving and stated retirement intentions of various age groups, see Employee Benefit Research Institute, *The 1997 Retirement Confidence Survey*.

4. Annamaria Lusardi, "Information, Expectations, and Saving for Retirement," paper presented to a conference on behavioral economics and retirement, sponsored by the Russell Sage Foundation, Stanford, Calif., April, 1998.

5. Support for the indigent may also promote excessively risky investment behavior by those with modest assets. Suppose that accumulated saving will provide a retirement income slightly greater than public aid if invested in a responsible mix of assets. One may be tempted to make a chancy investment with a small prospect of a big return, safe in the knowledge that if it succeeds, one reaps the gain, but if it fails one loses little, as one can fall back on public aid.

2

1. W. Andrew Achenbaum, *Social Security: Visions and Revisions* (New York: Cambridge University Press, 1986), p. 18; Edward O. Berkowitz, *America's Welfare State: From Roosevelt to Reagan* (Baltimore: Johns Hopkins University Press, 1991), p. 19.

2. By 1975, however, the law had been liberalized many times. Coverage was greatly extended in 1950. Disability benefits were added in 1956. Workers retiring in 1975 who had benefited from these and other liberalizations had not spent their full working lives paying taxes under the system from which they drew benefits. Accordingly, workers actually retiring in 1975 continued to receive benefits worth far more than the value of taxes they and their employers had paid.

3. Aid to Dependent Children (ADC) reimbursed states for a share of the costs they incurred providing welfare benefits to children living in fatherless families. It was renamed Aid to Families with Dependent Children (AFDC) in 1962 to reflect the fact that in 1950 the adult caregivers of these children became eligible for benefits. In 1996, the AFDC program was replaced with the Temporary Assistance to Needy Families (TANF) program.

4. Until the 1950s, reserves grew rapidly despite the policy change, because wages and employment grew rapidly during and after World War II and because benefits were not adjusted automatically for inflation. Starting in 1950, Congress periodically raised benefits by about the same amount that earnings increased, so that revenues, which were based on earnings, did not outpace benefits.

5. While the regular unemployment compensation program provides benefits for up to six months, Congress has often extended assistance for a year or more during periods of economic weakness.

6. Reduced Social Security benefits for those age 62 to 64 were made available to women in 1957 and men in 1962.

7. Frank Levy, *Dollars and Dreams: The Changing American Income Distribution* (New York: W.W. Norton & Co., 1988).

3

1. Whether workers' earnings grow steadily, rapidly at first and then slowly, or slowly at first and then rapidly will have a significant effect on the size of a defined-contribution pension relative to workers' final wages. Take, for example, three cases in which workers' earnings grew at an average rate of 5 percent over their forty-year careers. If earnings grew at 8.1 percent

during the first twenty years and 2 percent during the second twenty years, pensions would be 34 percent larger than if earnings grew at a steady 5 percent annual rate. And they would be 75 percent larger than pensions available if earnings grew at 2 percent for the first twenty years and 8.1 percent for the second twenty years. These estimates assume that contributions to the defined-contribution pension earned a steady 7 percent return per year.

2. Figure 3–1 shows the replacement rates—the ratio of benefits to the worker's average earnings between the ages of 54 and 58—for successive cohorts of hypothetical "average" male workers. The workers enter the labor force at age 22 and work for forty years. They experience the age-earnings profile of employed men in 1995. Economy-wide real earnings are assumed to grow 2 percent a year. Six percent of earnings are contributed to a defined-contribution pension plan that invests in a mixture of common stocks that yields the average dividend and capital gain of all listed securities in that year. The plan, which imposes no fees or charges, reinvests all dividends, which are free of individual tax when paid. At age 62, workers convert their accumulated savings into annuities based on the expected mortality experience of American men in 1995 and the interest rate on six-month commercial paper in the year when the annuity is purchased. All insurance company fees are ignored.

3. Take, for example, two workers with the same $58,997 average earnings over a forty-year period. One worker's annual earnings start at $30,000 and grow steadily by 3 percent a year. The other's start at $15,000 and grow at 5.8 percent a year. If each is required to contribute 5 percent of earnings to a defined-contribution plan that earns a steady 7 percent return per year, the pension of the first worker will be 28 percent larger than that of the second worker.

4. Government laws and regulations require insurance companies to charge some customers more for annuities and others less than available information on life expectancy warrants. Antidiscrimination laws prohibit race-based differences in annuity prices, even though whites are expected to live longer than blacks. At age 65, life expectancy of white males exceeds that of black males by two years. Accordingly, annuities for white men cost insurance companies more than do annuities sold to blacks. But law requires that the prices must be the same. The result is that blacks must systematically pay more and whites less than they would if annuity prices were based on average life expectancies. For some classes of insurance, prohibition of race-based price differences works in the opposite way. Blacks are almost twice as likely to become disabled as whites are. Disability insurance premiums based on race-specific disability rates would be higher for blacks than for whites, but such pricing is also prohibited. Gender may be used in setting prices for individual annuities. But it may not be used in determining pension amounts under group annuities.

5. Lawrence Thompson, *Older and Wiser: The Economics of Public Pensions* (Washington, D.C.: Urban Institute Press, 1998), pp. 155–59. The implicit inflation forecast over ten years is the difference between the annual yield to maturity on a ten-year bond and an estimate of the real rate of return. For example, ten-year Treasury index bonds that are fully protected against fluctuations in the consumer price index yielded approximately 3.5 percent in addition to the rate of inflation at the end of 1997. On August 6, 1998, for example, the interest rate on inflation-indexed Treasury bonds maturing in 2008 was 3.625 percent, while the interest rate on bonds without inflation protection was 5.625 percent, implying that investors expect inflation to average 2 percent a year over the succeeding decade. Thompson reports: "From the mid 1960s though the mid 1970s, many of the retirees relying on these market predictions would have ended up losing some 20 to 30 percent of their accumulated wealth to inflation not anticipated by the market. Losses would have been the smallest in Germany (averaging 14 percent from 1966 though 1973) and the largest in the United Kingdom (averaging about 76 percent from 1966 through 1973)."

6. Benefits are available to dependent children under the age of 18 and disabled dependent children age 18 or older.

7. Five members of the 1994–96 Advisory Council on Social Security proposed such a dual system. People who worked fewer than thirty-five years would receive a pro-rated portion of the flat benefit.

8. Social Security's income is composed of payroll tax receipts, a portion of the receipts derived from subjecting benefits above certain thresholds to the income tax, general fund transfers, and interest income on trust fund balances.

9. Returns for individual workers vary around this average for several reasons. The most important is that Social Security pays larger benefits relative to earnings to low earners and members of large families than to high earners and members of small families. If some people get more than average, someone must get less. In addition, projections are sometimes inaccurate. The changes in tax rates or pension rules necessary to reestablish financial balance alter returns of affected workers or pensioners. Congress sometimes adds new benefits—disability insurance in 1956, for example. When such changes occur, new beneficiaries enjoy temporarily inflated returns. They enjoy the same windfall that people who became eligible for benefits soon after Social Security was enacted received. In both cases, people become eligible for expanded benefits after only a brief period of paying the taxes to support those benefits.

10. As enacted in 1935, the Economic Security Act called for the imposition of payroll taxes starting in 1937 and the payment of retirement benefits starting in 1942. In 1939, Congress advanced to 1940 the date when benefits would first be paid. The 1935 law called for accumulation of reserves that

would have reached approximately twelve times annual benefit payments by 1970, a sizable reserve although well short of what would have been accumulated under a defined-contribution plan. The 1939 amendments moved Social Security to pay-as-you-go financing. That policy remained in effect until 1977, when legislation called for reserve accumulation to begin. The slowdown in trend economic growth that started in the mid-1970s spoiled those plans. Congressional action in 1983 initiated an era of reserve accumulation.

11. The adjustments could take place by rasing general revenues or curtailing spending elsewhere in the budget and transferring the resultant surplus to the retirement program.

12. We explore the likely effects of reserve accumulation on national saving in Chapter 5.

13. To the extent that Social Security encourages people to retire earlier than they would if Social Security did not exist, it stimulates saving. If people wish to maintain the same living standard after retirement that they enjoyed while working, increasing the duration of retirement raises the proportion of total lifetime income that will be consumed after earnings have stopped. To finance that consumption the portion of lifetime income consumed while working must be reduced—that is, saving has to increase. Many scholarly studies have addressed the question of whether, on balance, Social Security increases or decreases saving. The evidence is mixed.

14. Steve Stecklow and Sara Callian, "Financial Flop: Social Security Switch in U.K. Is Disastrous: A Caution to the U.S.?" *Wall Street Journal*, August 10, 1998, p. A1.

4

1. For the most part, the two groups are distinct. Most retired, disabled, and survivor beneficiaries do not work, but some engage in part-time work, and a few work full time. Overall, only 3.3 percent of beneficiaries have their pensions reduced or eliminated altogether because of earnings.

2. Robert M. Ball, "A Commentary on the Current Social Security Debate," unpublished paper, January 1998.

3. David M. Cutler and Ellen Meara, "The Medical Costs of the Young and Old: A Forty-Year Perspective," NBER Working Paper 6114, National Bureau of Economic Research, Cambridge, Mass., July 1997.

4. Over the 1990s, real per capita GDP grew at an average rate of 1.4 percent per year. Because the growth of the labor force is expected to slow more than population growth, the Congressional Budget Office, the Social Security Actuaries, and the Office of Management and Budget expect per capita growth to average 1.1 to 1.2 percent between 1998 and 2040.

5. Jonathan Gruber and David Wise, "Social Security Programs and Retirement Around the World," NBER Working Paper 6134, National Bureau of Economic Research, Cambridge, Mass., August 1997.

6. The age at which unreduced benefits will be paid rises two months a year starting for workers who turn age 62 in 2000 until it reaches 66 for those turning 62 in 2005. For the succeeding twelve years, the age of normal retirement will remain at 66. Then, it will be increased two months a year between 2017 and 2022. The increase in the "normal" age for claiming widows' and widowers' benefits begins and ends two years later.

7. There is no earnings test for those age 70 and older. Beneficiaries may receive unlimited amounts from private pensions, rents, royalties, and income from capital.

8. The cost of repealing the retirement test for those over age 64 would be modest because only a bit over half of those working and not receiving Social Security at this age will have earnings that exceed $30,000, the level the earnings test will reach in 2002. Furthermore, after 2005 when the delayed retirement credit fully compensates workers for benefits lost because of earnings above the threshold, the earnings test will have been effectively repealed. Repealing the earnings test means that workers receive the same expected lifetime benefits no matter when they retire. An actuarially fair delayed retirement credit has the same effect. However, the psychological effects of repealing the earnings test might well differ from those of an actuarially fair delayed retirement credit.

9. We explain why income testing is inadvisable in Box 7–1.

5

1. Social Security reserves were approximately $757 billion at the end of 1998—enough to support benefits for only about two years. Reserve accumulation is projected to continue until 2020, at which point reserves will be sufficient to pay for benefits for two and one-half years. Relative to benefits, reserves will peak in 2011, when they will be equal to about three and one-quarter years of benefits.

2. For example, some proposals would permit individuals to "opt out" of Social Security, that is, to shift their funds to personal retirement accounts. For reasons set forth in Box 3–6, such an approach is inherently unstable. The problem is that high earners would find it financially more attractive to leave Social Security than low earners would. While payroll taxes are proportional to earnings, benefits rise less than proportionally with earnings. In addition, high earners are more likely to be familiar with the operation of financial markets and would face proportionately lower administrative

charges because their private account balances would be larger. As a result, voluntary withdrawal would leave Social Security largely with low earners. Since low earners receive larger benefits in relation to their payroll tax payments than do high earners, voluntary withdrawal would create deficits, necessitating one of two responses. The payroll tax rate necessary to support benefits for workers who remain inside the system would have to rise, causing still more workers to withdraw. Or subsidies from general tax revenues would have to be provided to support the social assistance provided by the Social Security system. What this all means is that the proposal to permit workers to "opt" out of Social Security is not a complete plan. It buries the transition costs that most privatization plans honestly face by failing to analyze the inevitable consequences of permitting workers voluntarily to leave the system.

3. This represents the returns to the average wage worker, not the real return earned on the balances of the trust funds, which is estimated to be 2.8 percent over the long run.

4. If IRAs, Keogh plans, and the cash value of life insurance are excluded, fewer than one in eight families have liquid assets that exceed their annual income. Federal Reserve Board, *Survey of Consumer Finances*, Washington, D.C., 1995.

5. Caroline Daniel, "A Look at . . . The Future of Social Security: Taxing Reforms for British Retirees," *Washington Post*, Outlook, August 9, 1998, p. C3.

6. We assume that, subject to private (or public) offsets, described in the text below, the accumulation of funds in pension funds leads to smaller increases in consumption than do additions to income in other forms.

7. Almost all of the reserves are invested in special Treasury securities not sold to the public that have an important advantage. The Social Security trustees can sell their special issues to the Treasury at par regardless of the current market price of Treasury bonds of the same yield and maturity. This feature spares Social Security a risk that private investors face, of suffering a capital loss if compelled to sell bonds when interest rates were higher and bond prices lower than at issue.

8. B. Douglas Bernheim and Daniel M. Garrett, "The Determinants and Consequences of Financial Education in the Workplace: Evidence from a Survey of Households," NBER Working Paper 5667, Cambridge, Mass., July 1996; Patrick J. Bayer, B. Douglas Bernheim, and John Karl Scholz, "The Effects of Financial Education in the Workplace: Evidence from a Survey of Employers," NBER Working Paper 5655, Cambridge, Mass., July 1996.

9. Eric M. Engen and William G. Gale, "The Effects of Fundamental Tax Reform on Saving," in *Economic Effects of Fundamental Tax Reform*, edited by Henry J. Aaron and William G. Gale (Washington, D.C.: The Brookings Institution, 1996), Table 3–2, p. 86.

10. Peter D. Hart Research Associates, "Americans View the Social Security Debate," Washington, D.C., July 1998.

11. These estimates are drawn from Lawrence Thompson, "Risks of Mid-career Economic and Demographic Changes" (draft), September 23, 1997, for the International Social Security Association. Thompson's calculations show that the variability in contribution rates based on the experiences in Germany, Japan, and the United Kingdom would have been somewhat less extreme than those in the United States. Whether contribution rates would have to rise or fall depends on whether growth of wages is accelerating or decelerating and whether interest rates are rising or falling.

12. The costs of disability insurance, which are larger than those of retirement and survivor insurance, are not included in this figure because privatization plans typically do not encompass disability insurance.

13. Before 1995, the Social Security Administration provided reports only to those participants who requested information. As a result of legislation enacted in 1989 and 1990, SSA began sending information on past earnings and estimated benefits to all participants age 60 and older. By 2000, SSA will be required to provide information periodically to all workers age 25 and over who are not receiving benefits.

14. Olivia S. Mitchell, James M. Poterba, and Mark J. Warshawsky, "New Evidence on the Money's Worth of Individual Annuities," NBER Working Paper 6002, National Bureau of Economic Research, Cambridge, Mass., April 1997.

15. Such information would be needed if private account balances were divided upon divorce. If private accounts are treated as the sole property of the worker, divorced women could experience a substantial reduction in retirement incomes compared to the current situation.

16. One way to counteract this effect would be to impose a tax on funds not used to buy annuities, the proceeds from which would be used to subsidize annuities. The tax would offset the unfavorable selection into the annuity pool.

6

1. The figure is for 1997. In 1996, 12.3 percent of the elderly were poor after including Social Security income but before including other transfer payments. Other cash and in-kind government programs reduce the after-tax poverty rate for the elderly to 9.2 percent. These effects are measured net of Social Security payroll taxes, which reduce incomes and push some below the poverty threshold. Kathy Porter, Wendell Primus, Lynette Rawlings, and Esther Rosenbaum, *Strengths of the Safety Net*, Washington, D.C., Center on Budget and Policy Priorities, March 8, 1998, pp. 8, 30, Table A–2.

2. Jonathan Gruber and David Wise, "Social Security Programs and Retirement Around the World," NBER Working Paper No. 6134, National Bureau of Economic Research, Cambridge, Mass., August 1997, Table 1. The nations surveyed are Belgium, France, Italy, the Netherlands, the United Kingdom, Germany, Spain, Canada, the United States, Sweden, and Japan. We are not suggesting that the United States should emulate replacement rates or entitlement ages of other countries, which face burdensome growth of costs and will probably be forced to cut benefits. We are observing only that U.S. benefits are *relatively* modest.

3. A 1996 retiree who worked full-time at the minimum wage received an annual pension of $7,008 if single and $10,512 with a spouse's benefit. In 1996, the poverty threshold was $7,525 for a single person age 65 or older and $9,491 for a couple.

4. Because adjusting millions of pension benefits is a complicated task, the percentage increase in benefits provided in December of each year actually reflects inflation that occurred between the third quarter of the preceding year and the third quarter of the current year.

5. To be sure, work generates eligibility for disability coverage. An additional benefit is the "disability freeze," which shortens the worker's earnings averaging period for retirement benefits to the number of years already worked. These benefits are valuable, but they account for only a small share of the payroll tax.

6. The lower figure about equals the difference between the poverty threshold for an elderly couple and that for a single older person.

7. Some versions of earnings sharing credit each spouse with more than half of the combined total.

8. After ten years of marriage, divorced spouses are entitled to a spouse or survivor benefit, however far in the past the marriage may have ended. This provision means that a divorced person's pension can depend on the earnings record of a person the beneficiary has not lived with for two or even three decades.

9. Federal legislation enacted in 1984 requires that some fraction of the basic pension continue to be paid to the pensioner's widow or widower, unless he or she waives this right in writing.

10. Survivors receive the same benefit as the primary worker when their spouse dies. People who have been receiving a spouse's benefit or a worker's benefit smaller than the primary earner's receive the primary earner's benefit when he or she dies. The largest drop occurs when both spouses are entitled to the same benefit, each based on equal lifetime average earnings. The smallest drop occurs when one spouse receives the 50 percent spouse's benefit.

11. Conversely, age 67 retirees will not receive the increased benefits paid under the old law to people who work past age 65 and have sufficient earnings to be subject to the retirement test.

12. If in 2011, life expectancy at age 20 were 82.7 years, the number of years the average person lived beyond the age at which unreduced benefits were paid would be 15.7 (82.7 minus 67) and the retirement period would constitute one-quarter of adult life (82.7 minus 20). If average adult life expectancy were to increase by one year to 83.7, the age at which unreduced benefits were paid would rise to 67 years, nine months.

13. This is equivalent to a 62/3 percent reduction for each year before age 65 that benefits are claimed or an 81/3 percent (62/3 percent divided by 80 percent) increase in the pension for every year beyond age 62 that the worker delays applying for benefits.

14. Even if the benefit reduction rate for early retirement is actuarially sound, increasing the age of initial eligibility will reduce costs because those who die between the old and new age thresholds would receive no benefits.

15. Some have proposed extending the averaging period to 40 years, a change that would close over 20 percent of the projected long-term deficit. One variant of this proposal would count all lifetime earnings and divide the total by 40. This would boost benefits for those who worked steadily from when they were teenagers to when they retired. Any increase in the averaging period would reduce benefits for women and other groups that do not work continuously disproportionately.

16. The Congressional Budget Office has estimated that the changes adopted between 1995 and 2002 should reduce the growth rate of the CPI by about 0.7 percentage points a year. Congressional Budget Office, *The Economic and Budget Outlook, Fiscal Years 1999–2008* (Washington, D.C.: U.S. Government Printing Office, 1998), Box 1–2, pp. 8–9. See also Council of Economic Advisers, *The Economic Report of the President, 1998* (Washington, D.C.: U.S. Government Printing Office, 1998), pp. 79–80. For a thorough and accessible review of the issues, the best single source is the six articles in "Symposium: Measuring the CPI," *Journal of Economic Perspectives* 12, no. 1 (Winter 1998): 3–78.

17. The Omnibus Budget Reconciliation Act of 1990 required all state and local workers who were not covered by a pension plan to be in Social Security starting in July 1991.

18. Affected states and localities would have to modify their current pension plans, a manageable task that the federal government performed when its civilian employees hired after December 31, 1983, were brought into Social Security.

19. This estimate is based on the difference between the estimated long-run returns on government securities and private assets, not on the actual differences during 1998.

20. In fact, general revenues have been used in Social Security in limited ways. The allocation of revenues from income taxation of Social Security benefits is an application of general revenues. So also were payments made

to provide Social Security earnings credits for the military. In addition, when minimum Social Security benefits were eliminated in 1981, they were preserved for those born before 1920 and financed through a general revenue transfer.

21. The contribution depends on the other reforms because they generate larger reserves to invest.

22. This would take the form of a rule change that would establish a point of order requiring a sixty-vote majority to waive.

23. This law awarded the commissioner of Social Security a fixed six-year term. However, members of the president's cabinet continue to fill three of the six positions as Social Security trustees. We recommend that management responsibility for Social Security be placed under the Social Security Reserve Board, making it a truly independent institution modeled on the Federal Reserve system.

7

1. An appendix to the volume outlines several additional proposals.

2. Regulations could deal with this problem by stipulating that funds handling individual accounts would have to charge the same percentage of account balance on both large and small accounts. For recommendations along these lines, see Michael J. Boskin and Peter A. Diamond, eds., *Evaluating Issues in Privatizing Social Security: Report of the Panel on Privatizing Social Security* (Washington, D.C.: National Academy of Social Insurance, 1998).

3. This plan is described in Martin Feldstein and Andrew Samwick, "Two Percent Personal Retirement Accounts: Their Potential Effects on Social Security Tax Rates and National Saving," NBER Working Paper 6540, National Bureau of Economic Research, Cambridge, Mass., April 1998. A variant in which the government collects personal account contributions through payroll taxes, passes them on to private regulated fund managers chosen by workers, and requires annuitization of account balances upon retirement is presented in outline form in Martin Feldstein, "Testimony to the Senate Budget Committee," July 23, 1998.

4. The other plans examined could be more generous if they too used the projected budget surpluses—which amount to several trillions of dollars—to avoid benefit cuts.

5. These problems would be more manageable if the government used the payroll tax to collect deposits to personal retirement accounts, allocated them to the fund manager designated by the participant once a year, restricted investments to index funds, and required participants to annuitize their account balances upon retirement. Professor Feldstein suggested some of

these modifications in the outline he presented to the Senate Budget Committee on July 23, 1998.

6. Congressional Budget Office, "Analysis of a Proposal by Professor Martin Feldstein to Set Up Personal Retirement Accounts Financed by Tax Credits," August 4, 1998.

7. This estimate assumes that the worker's earnings grew at 1 percent a year in real terms until retirement, that the balances earned an average real return of 5 percent, and that annuitization was mandatory so there were no charges to compensate for adverse selection.

8. This plan was initially crafted by the National Commission on Retirement Policy, a group including members of Congress, leaders from the private sector, and policy analysts. An identical plan was introduced into the House of Representatives by Charles Stenholm (Democrat of Texas) and Jim Kolbe (Republican of Arizona).

9. Robert Ball has been associated with a number of proposals for closing the projected long-term deficit. Our comments here refer to the recommended Package 7 described in Robert M. Ball with Thomas N. Bethell, *Straight Talk About Social Security: An Analysis of the Issues in the Current Debate*, Century Foundation/Twentieth Century Fund Report (New York: Century Foundation Press, 1998).

10. Ball has pointed out that a defined-benefit plan could be supplemented by voluntary individual accounts at little additional administrative cost if such accounts were administered as payroll deductions and assets were managed by the Social Security Administration through a single pooled account. At retirement or disability, workers would have the option of withdrawing funds or converting their balances to annuities that would be added to their Social Security benefit. Robert M. Ball, "Social Security Plus," mimeo, July 1998.

11. Stephen C. Goss "Comparison of Financial Effects of Advisory Council Plans to Modify the OASDI Program," Report of the 1994–1996 Advisory Council on Social Security, Volume I, Findings and Recommendations (Washington, D.C.: Government Printing Office, 1997), p. 170.

12. Ball has also suggested that a Federal Reserve-type board be created to oversee reserve investment in equities. Robert M. Ball, "Social Security Plus."

Appendix

1. Committee for Economic Development, *Fixing Social Security: A Statement by the Research and Policy Committee of the Committee for Economic Development*, New York, 1997.

2. This plan was introduced in the 105th Congress as H.R. 2929, The Individual Social Security Accounts Act of 1997.

3. This plan was introduced in the 105th Congress as H.R. 2768, The Social Security Personal Retirement Accounts Act of 1997.

4. This plan was introduced in the 105th Congress as H.R. 3082, The Social Security Solvency Act of 1997.

5. Professors Kotlikoff and Sachs have published a number of similar plans. See Laurence J. Kotlikoff and Jeffrey Sachs, "It's High Time to Privatize," *The Brookings Review*, Summer 1997; "The Personal Security System: A Framework for Reforming Social Security," *Federal Reserve Bank of St. Louis Review* 80, no. 2, March/April 1998; and Laurence J. Kotlikoff, "Privatizing Social Security," National Center for Policy Analysis Report no. 217, Dallas, Tex., July 1998.

6. Many details of the Personal Security System plan have yet to be worked out. The principle of providing workers with the full accrued benefits under the old system is subject to widely varying interpretations, some of which could entail large increases in costs.

7. This plan was introduced in the 104th Congress as S.825.

8. Senator Phil Gramm, "Investment Based Social Security," 1998.

INDEX